CAMBRIDGE   SCHOOL

Shakespeare

Othello

Edited by Jane Coles

Series Editor: Rex Gibson
Director, Shakespeare and Schools Project

The right of the
University of Cambridge
to print and sell
all manner of books
was granted by
Henry VIII in 1534.
The University has printed
and published continuously
since 1584.

Cambridge University Press

Cambridge   New York   Port Chester
Melbourne   Sydney

Published by the Press Syndicate of the University of Cambridge
The Pitt Building, Trumpington Street, Cambridge CB2 1RP
40 West 20th Street, New York, NY 10011–4211, USA
10 Stamford Road, Oakleigh, Victoria 3166, Australia

First published 1992
Printed in Great Britain at the University Press, Cambridge

British Library cataloguing in publication data
Shakespeare, William, *1564–1616*
    Othello. – (Cambridge School Shakespeare).
    I. Title   II. Coles, Jane
    822.33

ISBN 0 521 39576 3 paperback

Library of Congress cataloguing in publication data applied for

Designed by Richard Morris
Illustrations by Jones and Sewell Associates
Picture research by Callie Kendall

Thanks are due to the following for permission to reproduce photographs:

Jacket: Study by Tony Armstrong Jones, Camera Press, London

20, From Giacomo Franco: *Habiti d'huomeni et donne Venetia*; 64, 183, British Home
Entertainment plc/photo: BFI; 88, Shakespeare Centre Library, Stratford-upon-
Avon; 91, 196, Philip Sayer; 108, 174, 233*r* and *b*, Richard Mildenhall; 112, 143*tr*,
Martha Swope Photography, Inc.; 132, Reg Wilson; 143*bl*, 231*r*, Billy Rose Theatre
Collection, New York Public Library at Lincoln Center, Astor, Lenox and Tilden
Foundations; 143*tr*, 233*l*, Raymond Mander & Joe Mitchenson Theatre Collection;
143*tl*, Bristol Theatre Collection/Photo: John Vickers: 231*l*, Harvard Theater
Collection; 237, The Shakespeare Institute, University of Birmingham.

*The editor and publisher would like to thank the following for permission to reproduce from
copyright material:*

Page 225 'White Lies' ('To whom it may concern') by Stanley Mogoba (South Africa,
1973), reproduced by permission of Ad Donker (Pty) Limited, Johannesburg, SA.
Page 226 'The Little Black Boy' by William Blake, reproduced from *Complete
Writings* (Oxford University Press, 1976), by permission of Oxford University Press.
Page 232 Extract from *The Noble Moor* by Helen Gardner, reproduced by permission
of the British Academy. *Proceedings of the British Academy*, Volume LXI, 1955. Page
233 Extract from *The Characters of Love* by John Bayley, published by Constable
Publishers. Extract from *Shakespeare* by Kiernan Ryan, published by Harvester
Wheatsheaf, reproduced by permission of the author. Extract from *Shakespeare* by
Germaine Greer (Oxford University Press, 1986), reproduced by permission of
Oxford University Press. Extract from 'Diabolic intellect and the noble hero' from
The Common Pursuit by F R Leavis, published by Chatto & Windus, reproduction by
permission of the Executors of the estate of F R Leavis.

Every attempt has been made to locate holders for all material in this book. The
publisher would be glad to hear from anyone whose copyright has been unwittingly
infringed.

Contents

Cambridge School Shakespeare

This edition of *Othello* is part of the *Cambridge School Shakespeare* series. Like every other play in the series, it has been specially prepared to help all students in schools and colleges.

This *Othello* aims to be different from other editions of the play. It invites you to bring the play to life in your classroom, hall or drama studio through enjoyable activities that will increase your understanding. Actors have created their different interpretations of the play over the centuries. Similarly, you are encouraged to make up your own mind about *Othello*, rather than having someone else's interpretation handed down to you.

Cambridge School Shakespeare does not offer you a cut-down or simplified version of the play. This is Shakespeare's language, filled with imaginative possibilities. You will find on every left-hand page: a summary of the action, an explanation of unfamiliar words, a choice of activities on Shakespeare's language, characters and stories.

Between each act and in the pages at the end of the play, you will find notes, illustrations and activities. These will help to increase your understanding of the whole play.

There are a large number of activities to give you the widest choice to suit your own particular needs. Please don't think you have to do every one. Choose the activities that will help you most.

This edition will be of value to you whether you are studying for an examination, reading for pleasure, or thinking of putting on the play to entertain others. You can work on the activities on your own or in groups. Many of the activities suggest a particular group size, but don't be afraid to make up larger or smaller groups to suit your own purposes.

Although you are invited to treat *Othello* as a play, you don't need special dramatic or theatrical skills to do the activities. By choosing your activities, and by exploring and experimenting, you can make your own interpretations of Shakespeare's language, characters and stories. Whatever you do, remember that Shakespeare wrote his plays to be acted, watched and enjoyed.

Rex Gibson

This edition of *Othello* uses the text of the play established by Norman Sanders in *The New Cambridge Shakespeare*.

List of characters

OTHELLO	A black army general in the service of the Duke of Venice
DESDEMONA	Othello's wife, daughter of Brabantio
IAGO	Othello's ensign (standard-bearer)
EMILIA	Iago's wife, companion to Desdemona
CASSIO	Othello's lieutenant
BIANCA	in love with Cassio

DUKE OF VENICE	
BRABANTIO	A Venetian senator, father of Desdemona
RODERIGO	A Venetian gentleman, in love with Desdemona
GRATIANO	Brabantio's brother
LODOVICO	Brabantio's relative

MONTANO	Governor of Cyprus

Senators of Venice
Gentlemen of Cyprus

CLOWN	Servant to Othello

Herald
Messenger
Musicians, soldiers, attendants, servants
Sailor

The action of the play takes place in Venice and Cyprus.

Two men are in the middle of an argument. Roderigo accuses Iago of cheating him. Iago is angry about failing to gain the promotion that has gone instead to Michael Cassio.

1 A dramatic opening (in pairs)

In the Elizabethan theatre there was no electric lighting and no stage curtain. The playwright had to signal the start of the play by means of a dramatic opening scene. Here, the noisy audience would be silenced by two men in the middle of a heated argument, with much swearing.

Read this opening conversation aloud (lines 1–34). Try reading it in several different ways to find which way sounds best. Share your final reading with the whole class – how many of you came up with the same ideas? Discuss which words in the script gave you clues as to how it should be spoken.

2 Key lines (in groups of four to six)

This is a lively and very noisy activity, but a fun way to start your studies on the play!

Both men have their own personal complaints to make. Search for key phrases or sentences in the script which seem to summarise their grumbles. Find two each and memorise them. Now stand opposite each other, at either side of the room. Walk towards each other shouting your lines. Try it again, making eye-contact with your partner as if you really hate them. Experiment with variations. Then talk together about the grievances your lines express.

3 What's gone before?

The play opens half-way through an argument. Make up what you think Iago and Roderigo have been saying *before* the play begins. End your dialogue on the first line of the play.

'Sblood by God's blood (a swearword)
suit attendance
bombast circumstance fancy excuse
Certes certainly

Florentine from Florence
devision strategical placing of soldiers
togèd consuls senators wearing the robes of peace

OTHELLO, THE MOOR OF VENICE

ACT I   SCENE I
Venice   A street at night

Enter RODERIGO and IAGO

RODERIGO Tush, never tell me, I take it much unkindly
    That thou, Iago, who hast had my purse
    As if the strings were thine shouldst know of this.
IAGO 'Sblood, but you will not hear me.
    If ever I did dream of such a matter,   5
    Abhor me.
RODERIGO Thou told'st me thou didst hold him in thy hate.
IAGO Despise me if I do not: three great ones of the city,
    In personal suit to make me his lieutenant,
    Off-capped to him; and by the faith of man,   10
    I know my price, I am worth no worse a place.
    But he, as loving his own pride and purposes,
    Evades them with a bombast circumstance,
    Horribly stuffed with epithets of war,
    And in conclusion,   15
    Non-suits my mediators. For 'Certes', says he,
    'I have already chosen my officer.'
    And what was he?
    Forsooth, a great arithmetician,
    One Michael Cassio, a Florentine,   20
    A fellow almost damned in a fair wife,
    That never set a squadron in the field,
    Nor the devision of a battle knows
    More than a spinster, unless the bookish theoric,
    Wherein the togèd consuls can propose   25
    As masterly as he. Mere prattle without practice
    Is all his soldiership. But he, sir, had the election,

Iago continues to complain about 'the Moor' and the system of promotion. He says he pretends to be a faithful officer, but follows Othello only to serve his own purposes.

1 What kind of man is Iago? (in small groups)

Read the page of script aloud several times, sharing out the lines.

On a large plain piece of paper write IAGO in the centre (see the diagram below) and collect together any **key** things Iago seems to say about himself. Include anything which reveals something about his character or motivation. On the outer layer of the diagram explain in your own words what each quotation indicates about him.

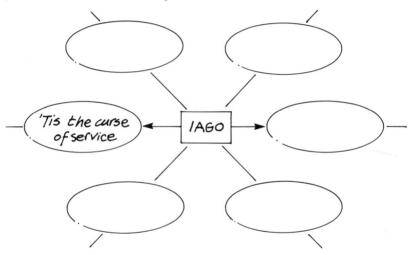

When you have finished, join together with other groups and compare your sheet with theirs. Explain how and why you chose your particular words/phrases/lines.

Pool your ideas together to produce one final diagram for display on your classroom wall.

---

lee'd pacified (sailing terminology)	**affined** bound
counter-caster accountant	**provender** food and drink
preferment promotion	**cashiered** dismissed from service
letter academic qualifications	**forms** outward shows
affection favouritism	**complement extern** outward show

And I, of whom his eyes had seen the proof
At Rhodes, at Cyprus, and on other grounds
Christian and heathen, must be lee'd and calmed   30
By debitor and creditor; this counter-caster,
He, in good time, must his lieutenant be,
And I, God bless the mark, his Moorship's ancient.
RODERIGO By heaven, I rather would have been his hangman.
IAGO Why, there's no remedy. 'Tis the curse of service;   35
Preferment goes by letter and affection,
Not by the old gradation, where each second
Stood heir to the first. Now sir, be judge yourself
Whether I in any just term am affined
To love the Moor.
RODERIGO   I would not follow him then.   40
IAGO O sir, content you.
I follow him to serve my turn upon him.
We cannot all be masters, nor all masters
Cannot be truly followed. You shall mark
Many a duteous and knee-crooking knave,   45
That doting on his own obsequious bondage,
Wears out his time much like his master's ass
For nought but provender, and when he's old, cashiered.
Whip me such honest knaves. Others there are
Who, trimmed in forms and visages of duty,   50
Keep yet their hearts attending on themselves,
And throwing but shows of service on their lords,
Do well thrive by them; and when they have lined their coats,
Do themselves homage. These fellows have some soul,
And such a one do I profess myself.   55
For, sir,
It is as sure as you are Roderigo,
Were I the Moor, I would not be Iago;
In following him, I follow but myself.
Heaven is my judge, not I for love and duty,   60
But seeming so for my peculiar end.
For when my outward action doth demonstrate
The native act and figure of my heart
In complement extern, 'tis not long after
But I will wear my heart upon my sleeve   65
For daws to peck at. I am not what I am.

Iago suggests a way of taking revenge against Othello. They shout in the street outside Brabantio's house and tell him the news that he has been 'robbed'.

1 'Brabantio appears above at a window' (in pairs)

Turn to page 186 where you will find an illustration of an Elizabethan theatre. It has a deep 'thrust' stage, with two exits at the back and a balcony above. Members of the audience stood crammed in 'the pit' all around the edges of the stage, sat in tiers of seating around the walls.

Talk together about how you would stage lines 68–93:

a on the Elizabethan stage

b on a modern acting space.

2 How do they speak to Brabantio? (in groups of three)

Read lines 68–143. Take parts. Notice the differences in the way the three characters speak. Do Iago and Roderigo take an equal share in giving information to Brabantio? When you have finished discussing, appoint an 'envoy' in your group who will go to another group in the room and share your findings with them.

Envoys – don't forget to take your copy of the script with you! You'll need to point to the actual words that characters speak in order to prove a point.

---

owe own
timorous frightening or fearful

tupping copulating with
snorting snoring

RODERIGO What a full fortune does the thick-lips owe,
  If he can carry it thus!
IAGO   Call up her father:
  Rouse him, make after him, poison his delight,
  Proclaim him in the street, incense her kinsmen,   70
  And though he in a fertile climate dwell,
  Plague him with flies: though that his joy be joy,
  Yet throw such chances of vexation on't
  As it may lose some colour.
RODERIGO Here is her father's house; I'll call aloud.   75
IAGO Do, with like timorous accent and dire yell,
  As when, by night and negligence, the fire
  Is spied in populous cities.
RODERIGO What ho, Brabantio! Signior Brabantio, ho!
IAGO Awake! What ho, Brabantio! Thieves, thieves!   80
  Look to your house, your daughter, and your bags!
  Thieves, thieves!

   BRABANTIO [*appears*] *above at a window.*

BRABANTIO What is the reason of this terrible summons?
  What is the matter there?
RODERIGO Signior, is all your family within?   85
IAGO Are your doors locked?
BRABANTIO   Why, wherefore ask you this?
IAGO Zounds, sir, you're robbed; for shame, put on your gown;
  Your heart is burst; you have lost half your soul;
  Even now, now, very now, an old black ram
  Is tupping your white ewe. Arise, arise;   90
  Awake the snorting citizens with the bell,
  Or else the devil will make a grandsire of you.
  Arise, I say!

Brabantio suspects the two men are drunk. He learns Roderigo's name,
but not Iago's. Iago obscenely tells him that Desdemona and Othello
are having sexual intercourse and that his descendants will be mere animals.

1 What's going on? (in pairs)

Imagine you are two servants in Brabantio's house, intrigued by the commotion outside. What can you make of the rag-bag of information shouted by the two men in the street? Improvise a 'below stairs' scene between the two servants.

2 Animals

Read through the script on pages 7 and 9. Pick out any references to animals or insects in the dialogue. It may help you to know that a 'Barbary horse' is a North African breed; 'coursers' are racehorses; and 'jennets' are a breed of small Spanish horse.

Write down which characters make the comments and what significance the choice of animal images has for you.

distempering draughts alcohol
start disturb
place position
grange house in the country

germans relatives
making the beast with two backs
  having sexual intercourse

BRABANTIO   What, have you lost your wits?

RODERIGO Most reverend signior, do you know my voice?

BRABANTIO Not I; what are you?   95

RODERIGO My name is Roderigo.

BRABANTIO   The worser welcome;
   I have charged thee not to haunt about my doors;
   In honest plainness thou hast heard me say
   My daughter is not for thee. And now in madness,
   Being full of supper and distempering draughts,   100
   Upon malicious bravery dost thou come
   To start my quiet.

RODERIGO Sir, sir, sir –

BRABANTIO   But thou must needs be sure
   My spirit and my place have in them power
   To make this bitter to thee.

RODERIGO   Patience, good sir.   105

BRABANTIO What tell'st thou me of robbing? This is Venice;
   My house is not a grange.

RODERIGO   Most grave Brabantio,
   In simple and pure soul I come to you.

IAGO Zounds, sir; you are one of those that will not serve God if the
   devil bid you. Because we come to do you service and you think   110
   we are ruffians, you'll have your daughter covered with a Barbary
   horse, you'll have your nephews neigh to you, you'll have
   coursers for cousins, and jennets for germans.

BRABANTIO What profane wretch art thou?

IAGO I am one, sir, that comes to tell you your daughter and the Moor   115
   are now making the beast with two backs.

BRABANTIO Thou art a villain.

IAGO   You are a senator.

Roderigo tells Brabantio that Desdemona has run away to live with Othello. Brabantio leaves to check if the story is true, saying he has already dreamt of such a happening.

1 Desdemona's flight (in groups of three)

Read Roderigo's report of Desdemona's secret departure from home (lines 119–36).

Mime her flight, using captions taken from Roderigo's story. Share your version with the rest of the class.

2 Parents' wishes and family rows

Even in Shakespeare's day young people rebelled against their parents. Desdemona has run away from home to marry a man of whom her father disapproves. Imagine the family rows that might have taken place before her marriage if only Brabantio knew. Choose one of the following and improvise a short scene:

a A family at home, late evening. One teenager is expected home any minute. There is a knock at the door. Neighbours bring news that they've seen the teenage daughter/son with a friend and a suitcase of clothes at the bus station . . . What happens next?

b A family dinner. In walks the teenage daughter with her 'disapproved of' boyfriend and announces they're getting married . . .

3 Venice

What are your first impressions of Venetian society as portrayed through the characters' words and actions so far? Make notes before comparing your ideas with other students. (See page 47 for more ideas about Venice.)

---

odd-even just after midnight
lascivious lustful
strike on the tinder make a light
taper candle

gall hurt
cast dismiss
loud reason strong support from the senate

BRABANTIO This thou shalt answer; I know thee, Roderigo.
RODERIGO Sir, I will answer anything. But I beseech you
    If't be your pleasure and most wise consent   120
    (As partly I find it is) that your fair daughter,
    At this odd-even and dull watch o'the night,
    Transported with no worse nor better guard,
    But with a knave of common hire, a gondolier,
    To the gross clasps of a lascivious Moor: 125
    If this be known to you, and your allowance,
    We then have done you bold and saucy wrongs.
    But if you know not this, my manners tell me,
    We have your wrong rebuke. Do not believe
    That from the sense of all civility   130
    I thus would play and trifle with your reverence.
    Your daughter, if you have not given her leave,
    I say again, hath made a gross revolt,
    Tying her duty, beauty, wit, and fortunes
    In an extravagant and wheeling stranger   135
    Of here and everywhere. Straight satisfy yourself.
    If she be in her chamber or your house,
    Let loose on me the justice of the state
    For thus deluding you.
BRABANTIO   Strike on the tinder, ho!
    Give me a taper; call up all my people.   140
    This accident is not unlike my dream;
    Belief of it oppresses me already.
    Light, I say, light!   *Exit*
IAGO   Farewell, for I must leave you.
    It seems not meet nor wholesome to my place
    To be produced, as if I stay I shall,   145
    Against the Moor. For I do know the state,
    However this may gall him with some check,
    Cannot with safety cast him; for he's embarked
    With such loud reason to the Cyprus wars,

Iago slips away, not wishing to be identified as a trouble-maker. Brabantio discovers his daughter is indeed missing. He goes off with Roderigo to seek assistance from neighbours and the police.

1 'The Moor' (in small groups)

Throughout the whole of this first scene, no one has used Othello's *name* – although all three men have referred to him several times. Collect all the terms used to describe Othello in Scene 1. Try to decide what aspect of Othello is being highlighted in each instance; is it a complimentary term or a derogatory one? Also, decide what these descriptive terms tell you about the *speaker* in each case.

Copy the following table and use it to record your findings:

Term used	Aspect of Othello	Spoken by?	What does it say about the speaker?
the Moor (40)	his race	Iago	He's trying to take away Othello's individuality
the thick-lips (67)	his physical features (stereotype)	Roderigo	Racist! Purposefully insulting
the devil . . .			

When you have completed your table, compare your ideas with those of other groups.

---

fathom capability
life livelihood, occupation
Sagittary the name of an inn
despisèd time time of great dishonour

charms spells, love potions
deserve your pains reward you for your trouble

Which even now stands in act, that, for their souls,   150
Another of his fathom they have none
To lead their business; in which regard,
Though I do hate him as I do hell's pains,
Yet, for necessity of present life,
I must show out a flag and sign of love,   155
Which is indeed but sign. That you shall surely find him,
Lead to the Sagittary the raisèd search,
And there will I be with him. So farewell.   *Exit*

Enter Brabantio in his nightgown, and SERVANTS *with torches.*

BRABANTIO It is too true an evil. Gone she is,
    And what's to come of my despisèd time   160
    Is nought but bitterness. Now Roderigo,
    Where didst thou see her? O unhappy girl!
    With the Moor, say'st thou? Who would be a father?
    How didst thou know 'twas she? O she deceives me
    Past thought! What said she to you? Get more tapers,   165
    Raise all my kindred. Are they married, think you?
RODERIGO Truly I think they are.
BRABANTIO O heaven! How got she out? O treason of the blood!
    Fathers, from hence trust not your daughters' minds
    By what you see them act. Is there not charms   170
    By which the property of youth and maidhood
    May be abused? Have you not read, Roderigo,
    Of some such thing?
RODERIGO   Yes, sir, I have indeed.
BRABANTIO Call up my brother. O that you had had her!
    Some one way, some another. Do you know   175
    Where we may apprehend her and the Moor?
RODERIGO I think I can discover him, if you please
    To get good guard and go along with me.
BRABANTIO Pray you lead on. At every house I'll call;
    I may command at most. Get weapons, ho!   180
    And raise some special officers of night:
    On, good Roderigo; I'll deserve your pains.
                                     Exeunt

Iago, pretending to be Othello's faithful supporter, warns Othello that Brabantio will attempt to break up the marriage. Othello is confident that his service to Venice and his noble descent will make all well.

1 Iago's version (in pairs)

In lines 4–10, Iago tells of the conversation he had with Roderigo. Talk together about how this version compares with what was actually said in the last scene.

2 First impressions of Othello

It is often said that first impressions are lasting impressions. Look closely at what Othello says in lines 17–28. What are your first impressions of Othello? Compare those first impressions with the descriptions given of him in Scene 1.

stuff essence
I lack . . . service sometimes I'm too nice for my own good
yerked stabbed
magnifico nobleman (Brabantio)
give him cable allow him

signiory the Venetian government
provulgate make public
siege rank
demerits deserts, worth
circumscription restriction

ACT 1 SCENE 2
Venice   Outside the Saggitary

Enter OTHELLO, IAGO and ATTENDANTS with torches

IAGO Though in the trade of war I have slain men,
　　　Yet do I hold it very stuff o'the conscience
　　　To do no contrived murder. I lack iniquity
　　　Sometimes to do me service. Nine or ten times
　　　I had thought to have yerked him here, under the ribs.　　5
OTHELLO 'Tis better as it is.
IAGO　　　　　　　　　Nay, but he prated,
　　　And spoke such scurvy and provoking terms
　　　Against your honour,
　　　That, with the little godliness I have,
　　　I did full hard forbear him. But I pray, sir,　　　　　10
　　　Are you fast married? For be sure of this,
　　　That the magnifico is much beloved,
　　　And hath in his effect a voice potential
　　　As double as the duke's. He will divorce you,
　　　Or put upon you what restraint and grievance　　　15
　　　The law, with all his might to enforce it on,
　　　Will give him cable.
OTHELLO　　　　　　　Let him do his spite;
　　　My services which I have done the signiory
　　　Shall out-tongue his complaints. 'Tis yet to know –
　　　Which, when I know that boasting is an honour,　　20
　　　I shall provulgate – I fetch my life and being
　　　From men of royal siege, and my demerits
　　　May speak unbonneted to as proud a fortune
　　　As this that I have reached. For know, Iago,
　　　But that I love the gentle Desdemona,　　　　　　　25
　　　I would not my unhousèd free condition
　　　Put into circumscription and confine
　　　For the sea's worth. But look what lights come yond!

Cassio arrives on an urgent mission from the Duke to find Othello. He reports that war is imminent and the senate urgently needs Othello. Iago tells Cassio of Othello's marriage.

1 Two-faced Janus (in pairs)

Why is it significant that Iago swears 'by Janus'? Stand back to back. One partner reads Iago's words in lines 1–53 aloud, pausing at the end of each sentence. The other partner speaks in each pause, saying what Iago's real thoughts might be.

2 Greetings (in groups of seven or more)

Two separate search parties come looking for Othello in lines 34–61, one on official war business, the other pursuing a personal grievance. Work out how each search party might enter and how they would greet Othello and Iago. Freeze each scene at the moment of greeting, making it clear from the way characters are looking or standing who they are, and what their intentions are. Show your two 'freeze-frames' (or tableaux) to the rest of the class. Can they guess who you are representing in each tableau?

3 'Boarded a land carrack'

When Cassio wonders why Othello is staying at the Sagittary, Iago tells him it is because Othello has 'boarded a land carrack' (taken a treasure ship by an act of 'land' piracy). Write down what you think Iago means by this cryptic comment, and how appropriate the choice of words seems to be.

---

raisèd search party (and indignant)
Janus a two-faced Roman god (January is named after him, as it faces back to winter and forward to summer)

divine guess
sequent one after the other

IAGO Those are the raisèd father and his friends;
        You were best go in.
OTHELLO   Not I; I must be found.   30
        My parts, my title, and my perfect soul
        Shall manifest me rightly. Is it they?
IAGO By Janus, I think no.

        Enter CASSIO, *with* OFFICERS *and torches.*

OTHELLO The servants of the duke and my lieutenant!
        The goodness of the night upon you, friends.   35
        What is the news?
CASSIO   The duke does greet you, general,
        And he requires your haste-post-haste appearance
        Even on the instant.
OTHELLO   What is the matter, think you?
CASSIO Something from Cyprus, as I may divine.
        It is a business of some heat. The galleys   40
        Have sent a dozen sequent messengers
        This very night at one another's heels;
        And many of the consuls, raised and met,
        Are at the duke's already. You have been hotly called for,
        When, being not at your lodging to be found,   45
        The senate hath sent about three several quests
        To search you out.
OTHELLO   'Tis well I am found by you.
        I will but spend a word here in the house,
        And go with you.   [*Exit*]
CASSIO   Ancient, what makes he here?
IAGO Faith, he tonight hath boarded a land carrack;   50
        If it prove lawful prize, he's made for ever.
CASSIO I do not understand.
IAGO   He's married.
CASSIO   To who?

        [*Enter Othello.*]

IAGO Marry, to – Come, captain, will you go?
OTHELLO   Have with you.
CASSIO Here comes another troop to seek for you.

*Brabantio abuses Othello and physically threatens him. He accuses
Othello of enchanting Desdemona with bad magic and drugs, and orders
his arrest. Othello reacts calmly.*

1 Othello's response (in pairs)

If you were directing a production of *Othello* what advice would you
give to the two actors playing Othello and Brabantio at line 57, 'Down
with him, thief!' and lines 59–61, 'Keep up your bright swords . . .'?
Experiment with ways of saying the lines and then explain to the rest
of the class how you came to make your decision.

2 Brabantio's speech (in groups of four)

Read lines 62–81. Pick out all the insulting terms Brabantio uses to
refer directly or indirectly to Othello. Next, take everything Othello
says opposite and divide it up into separate meaningful sections
(words, phrases, lines). Three of you share Brabantio's insults
between you, the fourth member of the group takes Othello's
language.

Explore ways of presenting your words or lines so that the
characters' relationships, moods and situation are clearly communicated.

3 What would you say? (in pairs)

If you were to insult someone in the same way as Brabantio insults
Othello, how would you expect that person to respond? Improvise a
modern equivalent situation. Think carefully about the way character
A insults character B and how B is likely to respond. Present your
improvisation to the rest of the class and talk together about the
variations.

---

keep up put away
refer me . . . sense appeal to
  common sense
guardage guardianship, safety of
  her home

gross in sense quite obvious
out of warrant against the law

Enter BRABANTIO, RODERIGO *and* OFFICERS *with lights and weapons.*

IAGO It is Brabantio; general, be advised,   55
    He comes to bad intent.
OTHELLO   Holla, stand there!
RODERIGO Signior, it is the Moor.
BRABANTIO   Down with him, thief!
IAGO You, Roderigo? Come, sir, I am for you.
OTHELLO Keep up your bright swords, for the dew will rust them.
    Good signior, you shall more command with years   60
    Than with your weapons.
BRABANTIO O thou foul thief! Where hast thou stowed my
        daughter?
    Damned as thou art, thou hast enchanted her,
    For I'll refer me to all things of sense,
    If she in chains of magic were not bound,   65
    Whether a maid so tender, fair, and happy,
    So opposite to marriage that she shunned
    The wealthy curlèd darlings of our nation,
    Would ever have, t'incur a general mock,
    Run from her guardage to the sooty bosom   70
    Of such a thing as thou – to fear, not to delight.
    Judge me the world, if 'tis not gross in sense
    That thou hast practised on her with foul charms,
    Abused her delicate youth with drugs or minerals
    That weakens motion. I'll have't disputed on;   75
    'Tis probable and palpable to thinking.
    I therefore apprehend and do attach thee
    For an abuser of the world, a practiser
    Of arts inhibited and out of warrant.
    Lay hold upon him. If he do resist,   80
    Subdue him at his peril.
OTHELLO   Hold your hands,
    Both you of my inclining and the rest.
    Were it my cue to fight, I should have known it
    Without a prompter. Where will you that I go
    To answer this your charge?
BRABANTIO   To prison, till fit time   85
    Of law and course of direct session
    Call thee to answer.

Brabantio is certain that the Duke will decide in his favour. In the next scene the Duke and Venetian Senators are considering news of the Turkish threats of war on Cyprus, a Venetian colony.

1 Setting Scene 3 – the Council Chamber

If you were directing this scene on stage what kind of room would you imagine it taking place in? Give reasons for your choice. Consider how you would show the change of location from the previous street scene on stage, using a bare minimum of props or music. Remember that in most modern productions, scene-changing is very swift indeed and one scene flows quickly into the next.

A contemporary drawing of the Duke (Doge) of Venice (1609).

---

brothers of the state fellow
  senators
composition agreement

jump not on a just accompt do
  not agree precisely
bearing up sailing towards

OTHELLO   What if I do obey?
     How may the duke be therewith satisfied,
     Whose messengers are here about my side
     Upon some present business of the state   90
     To bring me to him?
OFFICER   'Tis true, most worthy signior;
     The duke's in council, and your noble self
     I am sure is sent for.
BRABANTIO   How? The duke in council?
     In this time of the night? Bring him away;
     Mine's not an idle cause. The duke himself,   95
     Or any of my brothers of the state,
     Cannot but feel this wrong as 'twere their own;
     For if such actions may have passage free,
     Bondslaves and pagans shall our statesmen be.

                                                    Exeunt

ACT I   SCENE 3
Venice   The Council Chamber

Enter DUKE and SENATORS, set at a table with lights, and ATTENDANTS

DUKE There is no composition in these news
     That gives them credit.
I SENATOR   Indeed they are disproportioned.
     My letters say a hundred and seven galleys.
DUKE And mine, a hundred and forty.
2 SENATOR   And mine, two hundred;
     But though they jump not on a just accompt –   5
     As in these cases where the aim reports
     'Tis oft with difference – yet do they all confirm
     A Turkish fleet, and bearing up to Cyprus.

*Amid uncertainty about the size of the Turkish fleet, a sailor brings news
that it is now sailing towards Rhodes. However, a Senator and the
Duke agree that the Turks intend to attack Cyprus.*

1 The Mediterranean

In the sixteenth century, Venice was the dominant colonial force in
the Mediterranean. It was a thriving commercial centre. The powerful merchants protected their commercial empire with military
strength including mercenary forces. Cyprus was particularly valued
as a colony for being a profitable source of sugar and cotton.

2 Battle tactics (in small groups)

Prepare your own large scale maps of the Mediterranean, based on
the one above. Use it in a presentation of lines 14–46, pointing
appropriately as each speaker mentions a place.

---

secure me feel confident
approve accept
assay test

pageant show, diversion
brace readiness
wage risk

DUKE Nay, it is possible enough to judgement:
    I do not so secure me in the error,   10
    But the main article I do approve
    In fearful sense.
SAILOR *(Within)*   What ho! What ho! What ho!
OFFICER A messenger from the galleys.

Enter a SAILOR.

DUKE   Now, what's the business?
SAILOR The Turkish preparation makes for Rhodes;
    So was I bid report here to the state   15
    By Signior Angelo.
DUKE How say you by this change?
I SENATOR   This cannot be,
    By no assay of reason. 'Tis a pageant
    To keep us in false gaze. When we consider
    The importancy of Cyprus to the Turk,   20
    And let ourselves again but understand
    That as it more concerns the Turk than Rhodes,
    So may he with more facile question bear it,
    For that it stands not in such warlike brace,
    But altogether lacks the abilities   25
    That Rhodes is dressed in. If we make thought of this,
    We must not think the Turk is so unskilful
    To leave that latest which concerns him first,
    Neglecting an attempt of ease and gain
    To wake and wage a danger profitless.   30
DUKE Nay, in all confidence he's not for Rhodes.
OFFICER Here is more news.

A messenger from Montano, the Governor of Cyprus, brings more news: the Turkish fleet, reinforced, sails towards Cyprus. Discussion of war tactics is interrupted by Brabantio's and Othello's arrival.

1 Valiant Othello – the statue! (in pairs)

It has been common practice to erect statues to commemorate military leaders who have been considered to have performed 'great' deeds. One person becomes the sculptor, the other the 'raw material'. Create your own statue to commemorate 'Valiant Othello'.

2 Brabantio's grief (in small groups)

In lines 52–8, Brabantio is trying to convey the extent of his grief, and ends up using an image of a floodgate to do it. Do you think it is an appropriate image?

Either: create a graphic design based on lines 55–8; **or**: represent these lines, matching words with movement.

3 Public affairs and private anxiety (in small groups)

Brabantio says his 'particular grief' overcomes 'the general care' (matters of state). Some people claim he is being particularly selfish here. But what do you think? Talk together about whether Brabantio is being selfish, and whether 'particular grief' does always overwhelm 'the general care'.

Ottomites Turks (from the Ottoman Empire)
injointed linked up
engluts engulfs, overwhelms

Enter a MESSENGER.

MESSENGER The Ottomites, reverend and gracious,
      Steering with due course toward the isle of Rhodes
      Have there injointed with an after fleet.   35
1 SENATOR Ay, so I thought. How many, as you guess?
MESSENGER Of thirty sail, and now they do restem
      Their backward course, bearing with frank appearance
      Their purposes toward Cyprus. Signior Montano,
      Your trusty and most valiant servitor,   40
      With his free duty recommends you thus,
      And prays you to believe him.
DUKE 'Tis certain then for Cyprus.
      Marcus Luccicos, is not he in town?
1 SENATOR He's now in Florence.
DUKE   Write from us to him   45
      Post-post-haste dispatch.
1 SENATOR Here comes Brabantio and the valiant Moor.

Enter BRABANTIO, OTHELLO, CASSIO, IAGO, RODERIGO *and*
                  OFFICERS.

DUKE Valiant Othello we must straight employ you
      Against the general enemy Ottoman.
      [*To Brabantio*] I did not see you: welcome, gentle
         signior;   50
      We lacked your counsel and your help tonight.
BRABANTIO So did I yours. Good your grace, pardon me:
      Neither my place nor aught I heard of business
      Hath raised me from my bed, nor doth the general care
      Take hold on me; for my particular grief   55
      Is of so flood-gate and o'erbearing nature
      That it engluts and swallows other sorrows
      And yet is still itself.

Brabantio publicly accuses Othello of abducting and seducing his daughter. Othello offers to explain what has really happened.

---

1 Brabantio's story (in groups of four)

Present three moments from Brabantio's version of his daughter's flight, lines 59–64:

a 'the charm'
b 'the theft'
c 'the abuse'.

2 Othello's reply (in groups of four to six)

Read through Othello's speech, each person reading a small section and then handing over to the next person in the group. Once you've read it through once, try reading it round the circle in different styles or moods. Experiment with the sound of it until you can decide on the way which best fits the words.

3 Tableau – 'Here is the man' (in groups of seven or more)

At the precise moment Brabantio accuses Othello (line 71), there are at least seven characters on stage. Work out who they all are and discuss what you think might be going through each individual's mind. Then each person takes a character, decides on an appropriate reaction and works out where their character is placed in relation to the others.

Present it as a tableau (a frozen picture) to the rest of the class to guess who is who. After identification, the class can ask certain characters to step forward out of the tableau, and to reveal what their thoughts are at that moment.

---

of mountebanks from dubious dealers
sans without
bloody book of law laws including the death penalty

after your own sense however you want
our proper son my own son
pith strength
field battlefield
conjuration spells

DUKE   Why, what's the matter?

BRABANTIO My daughter! O, my daughter!

SENATORS   Dead?

BRABANTIO   Ay, to me.
　　　She is abused, stol'n from me, and corrupted   60
　　　By spells and medicines bought of mountebanks;
　　　For nature so preposterously to err,
　　　Being not deficient, blind, or lame of sense,
　　　Sans witchcraft could not.

DUKE Whoe'er he be that in this foul proceeding   65
　　　Hath thus beguiled your daughter of herself,
　　　And you of her, the bloody book of law
　　　You shall yourself read in the bitter letter
　　　After your own sense, yea, though our proper son
　　　Stood in your action.

BRABANTIO   Humbly I thank your grace.   70
　　　Here is the man: this Moor, whom now it seems
　　　Your special mandate for the state affairs
　　　Hath hither brought.

ALL   We are very sorry for't.

DUKE [To Othello] What in your own part can you say to this?

BRABANTIO Nothing, but this is so.   75

OTHELLO Most potent, grave, and reverend signiors,
　　　My very noble and approved good masters,
　　　That I have tane away this old man's daughter,
　　　It is most true; true I have married her;
　　　The very head and front of my offending   80
　　　Hath this extent, no more. Rude am I in my speech
　　　And little blessed with the soft phrase of peace,
　　　For since these arms of mine had seven years' pith
　　　Till now some nine moons wasted, they have used
　　　Their dearest action in the tented field;   85
　　　And little of this great world can I speak
　　　More than pertains to feats of broil and battle;
　　　And therefore little shall I grace my cause
　　　In speaking for myself. Yet, by your gracious patience,
　　　I will a round unvarnished tale deliver   90
　　　Of my whole course of love: what drugs, what charms,
　　　What conjuration and what mighty magic –
　　　For such proceedings I am charged withal –
　　　I won his daughter.

Brabantio again accuses Othello of drugging his daughter. The Duke asks for proof. Othello suggests Desdemona is sent for to give her side of the story. Iago goes to fetch her.

1 Prejudice (in small groups)

Part of the reason that Brabantio is so upset is because his daughter has married a man of a different colour. But are we today any more tolerant of so-called 'mixed-race' marriages?

Discuss what you think *your* family's reaction to you would be in a similar situation. Then think of any particular places or countries where other circumstances (political, religious) might create illicit relationships.

Improvise a short drama called 'Forbidden friendships'.

2 The case against Othello (in groups of five or more)

With all the talk of criminal acts and sentencing (for example, in 'the bloody book of law') it is almost as though Othello were on trial. What exactly is the 'case' against him?

Work out which of the characters on stage you would cast as judge, prosecutor, defendant, and witnesses. Choose a significant moment from the script and show where characters would be positioned on stage, in such a way as to illustrate the formality at a court trial of a serious offence. Each major character then summarises what they feel the main 'case' against Othello to be.

3 'Perfection' in a woman

According to Brabantio his daughter is a perfect mixture of womanly virtues. Gather from lines 94–8 the aspects he seems to admire in a woman. What is your opinion of his version of admirable female behaviour?

---

motion emotion, desires
credit reputation
dram potion
vouch assert

thin habits outward appearances
poor likelihoods weak possibilities
modern seeming common beliefs

BRABANTIO   A maiden never bold;
　　　Of spirit so still and quiet that her motion   95
　　　Blushed at herself; and she, in spite of nature,
　　　Of years, of country, credit, everything,
　　　To fall in love with what she feared to look on?
　　　It is a judgement maimed and most imperfect
　　　That will confess perfection so could err   100
　　　Against all rules of nature, and must be driven
　　　To find out practices of cunning hell
　　　Why this should be. I therefore vouch again
　　　That with some mixtures powerful o'er the blood
　　　Or with some dram conjured to this effect   105
　　　He wrought upon her.
DUKE   To vouch this is no proof
　　　Without more wider and more overt test
　　　Than these thin habits and poor likelihoods
　　　Of modern seeming do prefer against him.
I SENATOR But, Othello, speak: 110
　　　Did you by indirect and forcèd courses
　　　Subdue and poison this young maid's affections?
　　　Or came it by request and such fair question
　　　As soul to soul affordeth?
OTHELLO   I do beseech you
　　　Send for the lady to the Sagittary   115
　　　And let her speak of me before her father.
　　　If you do find me foul in her report,
　　　The trust, the office I do hold of you,
　　　Not only take away, but let your sentence
　　　Even fall upon my life.
DUKE   Fetch Desdemona hither.   120
OTHELLO Ancient, conduct them: you best know the place.
　　　　　　　　[*Exit Iago with two or three Attendants*]
　　　And till she come, as truly as to heaven
　　　I do confess the vices of my blood,
　　　So justly to your grave ears I'll present
　　　How I did thrive in this fair lady's love,   125
　　　And she in mine.
DUKE   Say it, Othello.

29

*Othello tells how he was introduced to Brabantio's household. He
recounts how his relationship with Desdemona began with her
fascination with the story of his life.*

1 Othello's history (in groups of four or five)

As a whole class, divide up Othello's summary of his life (lines
128–44) into sections. Each group chooses one of the incidents from
Othello's life and creates a short improvisation or a series of tableaux
based on their lines. Then put all the sections together.

Come back together as a class and show your collective version of
Othello's life history.

2 The courtship (in pairs)

Othello's account of his courtship of Desdemona gives a very
different picture of their relationship than that told by Brabantio.
Improvise two scenes between Othello and Desdemona, one taken
from Brabantio's version of events and the other illustrating how
Othello claims the courtship happened (lines 144–69).

Discuss which version you think is true, based on your impressions
of Brabantio and Othello.

3 'Rude in my speech'

Othello claims to be 'little blessed with the soft phrase of peace' (line
82). What do you think? Write a paragraph describing the way Othello
speaks and what it tells you about his personality.

---

chances events
by flood and field on sea and on
  land
antres caves

Anthropophagi man-eaters,
  cannibals
pliant favourable
intentively altogether

OTHELLO Her father loved me, oft invited me,
        Still questioned me the story of my life
        From year to year – the battles, sieges, fortunes
        That I have passed.   130
        I ran it through, even from my boyish days
        To the very moment that he bade me tell it;
        Wherein I spake of most disastrous chances,
        Of moving accidents by flood and field,
        Of hair-breadth scapes i'th'imminent deadly breach,   135
        Of being taken by the insolent foe
        And sold to slavery; of my redemption thence,
        And with it all my travels' history:
        Wherein of antres vast and deserts idle,
        Rough quarries, rocks, and hills whose heads touch
            heaven,   140
        It was my hint to speak – such was the process:
        And of the cannibals that each other eat,
        The Anthropophagi, and men whose heads
        Do grow beneath their shoulders. This to hear
        Would Desdemona seriously incline;   145
        But still the house affairs would draw her thence,
        Which ever as she could with haste dispatch
        She'd come again, and with a greedy ear
        Devour up my discourse; which I observing
        Took once a pliant hour and found good means   150
        To draw from her a prayer of earnest heart
        That I would all my pilgrimage dilate
        Whereof by parcels she had something heard,
        But not intentively. I did consent,
        And often did beguile her of her tears   155
        When I did speak of some distressful stroke
        That my youth suffered. My story being done,
        She gave me for my pains a world of sighs:

*Othello completes the story of his courtship just as Desdemona arrives.
Brabantio demands to know where her duty lies, and she answers
him diplomatically, but makes it clear that she now obeys
Othello before her father.*

1 'She loved me for the dangers I had passed'
(in groups of three of four)

Improvise a short scene using line 166 as the title. Experiment with
different styles of presentation, both serious and comic!

Afterwards, as a whole class, discuss whether you think this is a
sound foundation for a marriage. What is it, do you think, that
Desdemona is looking for in a man?

2 Desdemona's 'divided duty' (in pairs)

Brabantio directly challenges his daughter to say 'where most you owe
obedience'. Discuss whether you believe this to be a fair question and
to whom *you* feel you 'owe obedience' – if anyone.

On a large sheet of paper, create a design based on an image of
scales. Enter on each side of the scales what balanced argument
Desdemona gives in answer to her father's challenge. Add what other
items you think belong in each scale.

From the play so far, deduce what you can about the position of
women in Othello's society. Talk together about whether you think
daughters have an easier time of it today.

3 The effect of Othello's words

The Duke seems very impressed by Othello's story. He tells
Brabantio: 'Men do their broken weapons rather use/Than their bare
hands.'

What do you think is meant by this? Consider whether it seems to you
to be sound advice. Think of a situation which would illustrate the
Duke's words.

passing exceedingly
learn me teach me

She swore, in faith, 'twas strange, 'twas passing strange,
'Twas pitiful, 'twas wondrous pitiful;   160
She wished she had not heard it, yet she wished
That heaven had made her such a man. She thanked me,
And bade me, if I had a friend that loved her,
I should but teach him how to tell my story,
And that would woo her. Upon this hint I spake: 165
She loved me for the dangers I had passed,
And I loved her that she did pity them.
This only is the witchcraft I have used.
Here comes the lady: let her witness it.

Enter DESDEMONA, *Iago and Attendants.*

DUKE I think this tale would win my daughter too.   170
     Good Brabantio, take up this mangled matter at the best:
     Men do their broken weapons rather use
     Than their bare hands.
BRABANTIO   I pray you hear her speak.
     If she confess that she was half the wooer,
     Destruction on my head if my bad blame   175
     Light on the man! Come hither, gentle mistress;
     Do you perceive in all this noble company
     Where most you owe obedience?
DESDEMONA   My noble father,
     I do perceive here a divided duty:
     To you I am bound for life and education;   180
     My life and education both do learn me
     How to respect you. You are lord of all my duty;
     I am hitherto your daughter. But here's my husband;
     And so much duty as my mother showed
     To you, preferring you before her father,   185
     So much I challenge that I may profess
     Due to the Moor my lord.

Brabantio grudgingly gives up his accusations against Othello. The Duke attempts to cheer him up but Brabantio refuses comfort. The Duke appoints Othello to supreme charge of the defence of Cyprus.

1 Poor Brabantio? (in pairs)

Do you feel sorry for Brabantio? Re-read his lines 187–96 and 208–18.

If he were your father, how would you feel at this moment? Identify which of his words might have the greatest effect on you (moving you to anger, pity or regret, etc.). Talk together with your partner about your reactions.

2 Proverbs and clichés (in groups of three)

The Duke sounds a little like an Elizabethan agony aunt! He speaks a series of clichés and proverbs (along the lines of 'every cloud has a silver lining'). Read aloud lines 200–07 to hear what it sounds like. Pick out the three distinct pieces of advice he gives to Brabantio.

Now, improvise a radio phone-in where an agony aunt gives advice to a modern-day father like Brabantio, and also gives advice to his daughter. (You might incorporate a few modern clichés or proverbs into the agony aunt's reply.)

3 Back to business

The Duke stops speaking in verse when he begins to discuss affairs of state. If you were directing this scene, how would you mark this change on stage (e.g. in tone of voice, movement, position of characters, etc.)?

God bu'y God be with you! (goodbye!)
clogs blocks of wood tied to horses' legs to stop them escaping
grise step on a staircase

the robbed a person who has been robbed
bootless useless
gall bitterness
slubber spoil

BRABANTIO   God bu'y! I have done.
    Please it your grace, on to the state affairs.
    I had rather to adopt a child than get it.
    Come hither, Moor: 190
    I here do give thee that with all my heart
    Which, but thou hast already, with all my heart
    I would keep from thee. For your sake, jewel,
    I am glad at soul I have no other child,
    For thy escape would teach me tyranny   195
    To hang clogs on them. I have done, my lord.
DUKE Let me speak like yourself and lay a sentence
    Which as a grise or step may help these lovers
    Into your favour.
    When remedies are past the griefs are ended   200
    By seeing the worst which late on hopes depended.
    To mourn a mischief that is past and gone
    Is the next way to draw new mischief on.
    What cannot be preserved when fortune takes,
    Patience her injury a mockery makes.   205
    The robbed that smiles steals something from the thief;
    He robs himself that spends a bootless grief.
BRABANTIO So let the Turk of Cyprus us beguile,
    We lose it not so long as we can smile;
    He bears the sentence well that nothing bears   210
    But the free comfort which from thence he hears;
    But he bears both the sentence and the sorrow
    That to pay grief must of poor patience borrow.
    These sentences, to sugar or to gall,
    Being strong on both sides, are equivocal.   215
    But words are words; I never yet did hear
    That the bruisèd heart was piercèd through the ear.
    Beseech you now, to the affairs of the state.
DUKE The Turk with a most mighty preparation makes for Cyprus.
    Othello, the fortitude of the place is best known to you; and   220
    though we have there a substitute of most allowed sufficiency,
    yet opinion, a more sovereign mistress of effects, throws a
    more safer voice on you. You must therefore be content to
    slubber the gloss of your new fortunes with this more stubborn
    and boisterous expedition.   225

Othello pledges his prompt departure to Cyprus, asking only that Desdemona be provided for. Neither Brabantio nor Othello nor Desdemona wishes her to return to her father's house. Desdemona asks if she might accompany Othello.

1 'I saw Othello's visage in his mind' (in pairs)

Spend five minutes discussing what you think Desdemona means by line 248. Can you decide why she feels it important to make the point at this moment?

2 'A maiden never bold'?

Remember, Desdemona's father said of her:

'A maiden never bold;
Of spirit so still and quiet that her motion
Blushed at herself.'
(Act 1, Scene 3 lines 94–6)

How well does her father really know her?

Re-read the opposite page from line 232. Make notes on what you understand to be the conventional thing for a woman to do in these circumstances. Do you think that Desdemona conforms to these conventions? Think about all of Desdemona's actions in the play so far. Try to decide what kind of a woman she appears to be. Don't forget to find evidence for your ideas.

3 'Storm of fortunes' (in pairs)

This comment at line 245 by Desdemona may mean either 'taking my future by storm' or 'creating a stormy future'. One edition of the play uses the word 'scorn' instead of 'storm', so that she is saying that she loves Othello so much she has sacrificed her secure family life for him. Talk together about whether you think 'storm' or 'scorn' is most appropriate and why.

---

thrice-driven bed of down a feather bed of the very finest quality
agnise acknowledge
Ottomites Turks

disposition arrangements
exhibition financial support
besort servants
downright violence open rebellion

OTHELLO The tyrant custom, most grave senators,
    Hath made the flinty and steel couch of war
    My thrice-driven bed of down. I do agnise
    A natural and prompt alacrity
    I find in hardness, and do undertake   230
    These present wars against the Ottomites.
    Most humbly, therefore, bending to your state,
    I crave fit disposition for my wife,
    Due reference of place and exhibition
    With such accommodation and besort   235
    As levels with her breeding.
DUKE   If you please,
    Be't at her father's.
BRABANTIO   I'll not have it so.
OTHELLO Nor I.
DESDEMONA   Nor I; I would not there reside
    To put my father in impatient thoughts
    By being in his eye. Most gracious duke,   240
    To my unfolding lend your prosperous ear
    And let me find a charter in your voice
    T'assist my simpleness.
DUKE   What would you, Desdemona?
DESDEMONA That I did love the Moor to live with him,
    My downright violence and storm of fortunes   245
    May trumpet to the world. My heart's subdued
    Even to the very quality of my lord.
    I saw Othello's visage in his mind
    And to his honours and his valiant parts
    Did I my soul and fortunes consecrate.   250
    So that, dear lords, if I be left behind
    A moth of peace, and he go to the war,
    The rites for which I love him are bereft me,
    And I a heavy interim shall support
    By his dear absence. Let me go with him.   255

Strange for woman at the time. Differs from her fathers description.

Othello wishes Desdemona to accompany him, and asserts that she will not distract him from his military duties. The Duke orders that they must depart that very night for Cyprus. Brabantio warns Othello of Desdemona's deceit.

1 'To be free and bounteous to her mind'

The meaning of lines 257–61 seems to be that Othello wants Desdemona's company for her mind, not her body ('not to please the palate of my appetite'). Do you think it's important that Othello explains his motives at this point?

2 'Let housewives make a skillet of my helm' (in pairs)

Othello assures the senators that he will not be distracted by Desdemona's presence. In lines 262–70 he uses two images to underline his assertion: firstly, that of Cupid blindfolding him, and secondly, his helmet converted to a cooking pot (skillet). Locate the exact words, then design a visual representation of both images.

3 'A man he is of honesty and trust' (in small groups)

Line 280 is an example of **dramatic irony**, where the audience knows more than a character on stage. There are numerous examples of it in *Othello*. Talk together about the dramatic effect of such lines.

4 A 'fair' comment?

The Duke comments: 'If virtue no delighted beauty lack,/Your son-in-law is far more fair than black.'

This is meant to be a compliment about Othello! Jot down what you think Othello might have replied to this comment if he had had the opportunity. (See page 224 for an activity on the word 'black'.)

---

scant neglect
seel close up
disports sexual pleasures
indign unworthy

make head against attack
estimation reputation
import concern

OTHELLO Let her have your voice.
    Vouch with me, heaven, I therefore beg it not
    To please the palate of my appetite,
    Nor to comply with heat the young affects
    In my distinct and proper satisfaction,   260
    But to be free and bounteous to her mind.
    And heaven defend your good souls that you think
    I will your serious and great business scant
    For she is with me. No, when light-winged toys
    Of feathered Cupid seel with wanton dullness   265
    My speculative and officed instruments,
    That my disports corrupt and taint my business,
    Let housewives make a skillet of my helm,
    And all indign and base adversities
    Make head against my estimation!   270
DUKE Be it as you shall privately determine,
    Either for her stay or going. Th'affair cries haste,
    And speed must answer it. You must hence tonight.
DESDEMONA Tonight, my lord?
DUKE   This night.
OTHELLO   With all my heart.
DUKE At nine i'the morning, here we'll meet again.   275
    Othello, leave some officer behind
    And he shall our commission bring to you
    With such things else of quality and respect
    As doth import you.
OTHELLO   So please your grace, my ancient:
    A man he is of honesty and trust.   280
    To his conveyance I assign my wife,
    With what else needful your good grace shall think
    To be sent after me.
DUKE   Let it be so.
    Good night to everyone. [*To Brabantio*] And noble
        signior,
    If virtue no delighted beauty lack,   285
    Your son-in-law is far more fair than black.
1 SENATOR Adieu, brave Moor; use Desdemona well.
BRABANTIO Look to her, Moor, if thou hast eyes to see:
    She has deceived her father and may thee.
OTHELLO My life upon her faith!
    Exeunt [Duke, Brabantio, Cassio, Senators and Attendants]

*Othello charges Iago to look after Desdemona. Roderigo is despondent
but Iago scorns his love-sickness and argues that will and reason
govern men's appetites.*

1 Roderigo and Iago (in groups of three)

Read the exchange between Iago and Roderigo, then try different
ways of acting it out. The third member of the group is the director.
Can you distinguish between the two characters in the way you
present it? (Remember, Roderigo is a 'gentleman', whilst Iago is a
professional soldier.) Try reading it in a variety of styles (e.g. serious,
funny, threatening, etc.). Which one sounds best?

2 Iago's garden imagery (in pairs)

Writers use **imagery** to help create an 'image' or picture in the
reader's or listener's mind. Garden imagery is used by Shakespeare
in other plays too (for example in *King Richard II* the whole kingdom
is likened to an unkempt garden). How successful is Iago at creating a
picture for you and does it help make clearer what he is saying to
Roderigo?

Talk with your partner about whether you agree with Iago's view
that 'our wills are gardeners' where our emotions are concerned, and
that love is 'a sect or scion' (grafted on). Can love be controlled by
reason?

3 Sexist language

Some readers find the terms Iago uses to describe women to be highly
offensive. For example, derogatory terms like 'guinea-hen' (a 'tart'),
and his exclamations of 'a fig!' – a contemptuous remark usually
accompanied by making a rude gesture (thrusting the thumb between
the first and second fingers). Why do you think Iago uses sexist
language?

---

incontinently immediately
gender type
corrigible authority ability to
  control

poise counterbalance
unbitted unbridled

Honest Iago

My Desdemona must I leave to thee;
I prithee, let thy wife attend on her,
And bring her after in the best advantage.
Come, Desdemona, I have but an hour
Of love, of worldly matters and direction   295
To spend with thee. We must obey the time.

Exeunt Othello and Desdemona

RODERIGO Iago.
IAGO What say'st thou, noble heart?
RODERIGO What will I do, think'st thou?
IAGO Why, go to bed and sleep.   300
RODERIGO I will incontinently drown myself.
IAGO If thou dost, I shall never love thee after. Why, thou silly
    gentleman?
RODERIGO It is silliness to live, when to live is torment: and then we
    have a prescription to die, when death is our physician.   305
IAGO O villainous! I have looked upon the world for four times seven
    years, and since I could distinguish betwixt a benefit and an
    injury, I never found a man that knew how to love himself. Ere
    I would say I would drown myself for the love of a guinea-hen,
    I would change my humanity with a baboon.   310
RODERIGO What should I do? I confess it is my shame to be so fond,
    but it is not in my virtue to amend it.
IAGO Virtue? A fig! 'Tis in ourselves that we are thus or thus. Our
    bodies are our gardens, to the which our wills are gardeners. So
    that if we will plant nettles or sow lettuce, set hyssop and weed   315
    up thyme, supply it with one gender of herbs or distract it
    with many, either to have it sterile with idleness or manured with
    industry, why the power and corrigible authority of this lies in
    our wills. If the balance of our lives had not one scale of reason
    to poise another of sensuality, the blood and baseness of our   320
    natures would conduct us to most preposterous conclusions. But
    we have reason to cool our raging motions, our carnal stings,
    our unbitted lusts; whereof I take this, that you call love, to be
    a sect or scion.
RODERIGO It cannot be.   325

Othello

Iago continues to persuade Roderigo that Desdemona and Othello will soon tire of one another. He tells of his hatred for Othello and urges Roderigo to join him in seeking revenge.

1 Iago's speeches (in groups of eight)

Form a circle and read through Iago's two speeches opposite. Read a sentence each in turn, around the circle.

Experiment with different ways of reading and presenting the speeches. You could try forming a straight line with everyone facing the same way; then, on saying a line turn and face the person behind, quickly one after the other. Find which actions suit the words best.

2 Love or lust? (in groups of four)

Look back over Iago's speeches on the previous page and the page opposite. What seems to be his attitude to human relationships? How would you sum up his philosophy on life?

Now find what you believe to be six *key* sentences or phrases. (spend at least fifteen minutes doing this). When you are in agreement, find ways of presenting those key lines, either through drama, or by making posters or some other form of presentation.

As a whole class share each presentation. Talk together about the differences which occur.

perdurable long lasting
stead help
sequestration separation
locusts fruits of the carob tree

acerb bitter
coloquintida bitter apple
conjunctive allied
Traverse! About turn!

IAGO It is merely a lust of the blood and a permission of the will. Come, be a man. Drown thyself? Drown cats and blind puppies. I have professed me thy friend, and I confess me knit to thy deserving with cables of perdurable toughness. I could never better stead thee than now. Put money in thy purse. Follow 330 thou these wars; defeat thy favour with an usurped beard. I say, put money in thy purse. It cannot be that Desdemona should long continue her love to the Moor – put money in thy purse – nor he his to her. It was a violent commencement, and thou shalt see an answerable sequestration – put but money in thy 335 purse. These Moors are changeable in their wills – fill thy purse with money. The food that to him now is as luscious as locusts shall be to him shortly as acerb as the coloquintida. She must change for youth; when she is sated with his body she will find the error of her choice. Therefore put money in thy 340 purse. If thou wilt needs damn thyself, do it a more delicate way than drowning. Make all the money thou canst. If sanctimony and a frail vow betwixt an erring barbarian and a super-subtle Venetian be not too hard for my wits and all the tribe of hell, thou shalt enjoy her – therefore make money. A pox of drowning 345 thyself! It is clean out of the way. Seek thou rather to be hanged in compassing thy joy than to be drowned and go without her.

RODERIGO Wilt thou be fast to my hopes, if I depend on the issue?

IAGO Thou art sure of me. Go make money. I have told thee often, and I retell thee again and again, I hate the Moor. My cause is 350 hearted: thine hath no less reason. Let us be conjunctive in our revenge against him. If thou canst cuckold him, thou dost thyself a pleasure, me a sport. There are many events in the womb of time which will be delivered. Traverse! Go, provide thy money. We will have more of this tomorrow. Adieu. 355

RODERIGO Where shall we meet i'the morning?

IAGO At my lodging.

RODERIGO I'll be with thee betimes.

IAGO Go to; farewell. Do you hear, Roderigo?

RODERIGO What say you? 360

IAGO No more of drowning, do you hear?

RODERIGO I am changed.

IAGO Go to; farewell. Put money enough in your purse.

RODERIGO I'll sell all my land. *Exit*

Iago is left alone on stage. He reveals that he suspects his wife has been unfaithful with Othello. He begins to make plans to ruin Othello's marriage and to seek revenge on Cassio, by making Othello believe Cassio and Desdemona are lovers.

1 Iago's soliloquy

The **soliloquy** is a dramatic convention. A character who is alone on stage speaks his or her own thoughts aloud. On the Elizabethan and Jacobean stages it is likely that the speech was addressed from the front of the stage directly to the audience.

Usually, the soliloquy reveals a character's thoughts, motives or state of mind at that point in the play.

This is the first time Iago has been alone on stage. It is the first time the audience has had the opportunity to hear his version of events. Three ways in which a director could present this speech are:

a directed towards the audience

b as if Iago is talking to himself

c as a voice-over, whilst the actor looks pensive and lost in thought. This method has been used in film and television versions of Shakespeare plays.

Read the speech in each of the three ways listed above. Consider for each method:

- how the actor would speak the lines
- what movements would be required
- in what differing ways you wish the audience to react
- how it affects your interpretation of Iago's character: sly, evil or manipulative? Does it draw the audience into colluding and sympathising with Iago?

Make notes on each version as you try it out. Report back to the rest of the class.

---

snipe a long-beaked bird (but here a derogatory term)
abroad generally
done my office slept with my wife
proper handsome

plume up my will have a bit of fun, or glorify myself
framed made
engendered formed, created

44

IAGO Thus do I ever make my fool my purse;   365
      For I mine own gained knowledge should profane
      If I would time expend with such a snipe
      But for my sport and profit. I hate the Moor,
      And it is thought abroad that 'twixt my sheets
      He's done my office. I know not if't be true   370
      Yet I, for mere suspicion in that kind,
      Will do as if for surety. He holds me well:
      The better shall my purpose work on him.
      Cassio's a proper man: let me see now;
      To get his place and to plume up my will   375
      In double knavery. How? How? Let's see.
      After some time, to abuse Othello's ear
      That he is too familiar with his wife;
      He hath a person and a smooth dispose
      To be suspected, framed to make women false.   380
      The Moor is of a free and open nature,
      That thinks men honest that but seem to be so,
      And will as tenderly be led by the nose
      As asses are.
      I have't. It is engendered. Hell and night   385
      Must bring this monstrous birth to the world's light.   *Exit*

The story so far . . .
Looking back at Act 1

1 Cast the play (in pairs)

Imagine you are a film director about to put together a new and exciting version of *Othello*. Go through the cast list on page 1, noting down those characters you have encountered in Act 1. Decide which well-known film actors you would cast in each part – money no object! In each case, say what it is about that particular actor which leads you to believe they are right for the part.

2 'Letter and affection' (in groups of four)

In the opening lines of the play Iago said that 'three great ones of the city' had canvassed on his behalf for promotion to Lieutenant. What went wrong? If Othello's 'ancient' is 'a man of honesty and trust', why didn't Iago get the job? Improvise the exchanges between the three Venetians and Othello. What reasons does Othello give for preferring Cassio? (See Act 1, Scene 1, lines 8–39).

3 Quotations (in groups of six)

Choose one each of the following quotations: (all taken from Act 1):
'my life upon her faith'
'she has deceived her father and may thee'
'I am not what I am'
'I must show out a flag and sign of love'
'trust not your daughters' minds/By what you see them act'
'I do perceive here a divided duty'.

Create an improvisation which incorporates each person's line – it need not have anything to do with *Othello*. (Feel free to split up lines and repeat them as much as you like.)

Why does Shakespeare set Act 1 in Venice?

One answer would be that Shakespeare's source story is set in Venice and Cyprus, and he simply copied it – but that's not the only answer. It's important to know something about sixteenth-century Venice and its social and economic significance in Europe, because places carry associations which may affect the way we interpret people or events.

For example, if you were to write a modern play involving a marriage between a black man and a white woman, it would make a huge difference if you chose to set it in South Africa's Johannesburg rather than, say, in New York. For a late twentieth-century audience the very name Johannesburg cannot fail to raise certain political and social expectations. The 'story' cannot be separated from its context.

So Venice carried certain associations?

For an English audience in 1604 (when the play was first performed), Venice was a byword for thriving capitalism. It was a republic where the wealthier merchant classes controlled the state, buying powerful military forces to protect their colonial exploits. In contrast, England had only just started increasing overseas trade in Africa, India and elsewhere, and was on the brink of massive colonial enterprise in the 'New World'. English merchants would recognise in Venice the mercantile and colonial force that they would like to see England become.

And in the terms of the play . . . ?

The Venetian State employed mercenary soldiers. It was a cosmopolitan state, so a black military leader would not be unusual. Othello, an ex-slave, is revered by the Venetian Senate simply because he very effectively, defends their interests. He is, however, not entirely 'one of them' (as Brabantio makes clear) when it comes to marrying one of their daughters. Desdemona is described in terms of stolen jewellery precisely because Brabantio feels he has been robbed – by someone who was employed to *protect* his possessions! The non-feudal society of Venice confers *power* on Othello, but not *status*. This provides a rich source of dramatic tension.

In Act 1, Venetian law and order is seen to operate quickly and efficiently. Iago's trouble-making is easily dealt with, as is the Turkish threat to Venetian stability. But . . . as you go into Act 2 remember we are moving to a disputed outpost on the edges of Venetian rule. Our introduction to Cyprus is a violent storm where the natural boundaries between sea and sky are blurred.

Montano and two Gentlemen discuss the terrible storm. A third Gentleman brings news that the Turkish fleet has been destroyed. He reports that Cassio's ship has safely docked, but that Othello is still at sea.

1 Setting (in pairs)

As with most Elizabethan drama, there are no original stage directions for this scene specifying where it takes place. How would an audience know who these people are in this opening scene of Act 2? Read the dialogue opposite and pick out any clues as to setting and characters.

Imagine you are directors of a production of *Othello*. Write notes on how you would stage this page of script, and what directions you would give the actors. Your aim is to help the audience to understand where they are and what is going on.

2 The storm

In the original story by Giraldi Cinthio, from which Shakespeare took his ideas for *Othello*, there is no storm at all, yet we have here a whole page of dialogue devoted to a description of it. You will also find that in the next few pages most of the characters will mention the storm several times. Presumably Shakespeare considered a storm at this point would have some dramatic or thematic use.

Some commentators suggest that the storm has a symbolic function ('the calm before the storm . . .', 'stormy emotions . . .', and so on). Can you think of other similar sayings?

At the end of this act (see page 90) you will be invited to look at this matter of the storm in more detail. As you read the rest of this scene be aware of the storm and its effects.

---

descry make out, see
ribs of oak of a boat
hold the mortise hold their joints
 together
banning forbidding

chidden billow waves hurled back
Bear/Pole constellation of stars
 (*Ursa Major*) and the pole star
Veronesa Italian ship

ACT 2 SCENE 1
Cyprus   A quayside

Enter MONTANO *and two* GENTLEMEN

MONTANO What from the cape can you discern at sea?

1 GENTLEMAN Nothing at all; it is a high-wrought flood.
    I cannot 'twixt the heaven and the main
    Descry a sail.

MONTANO Methinks the wind does speak aloud at land,   5
    A fuller blast ne'er shook our battlements.
    If it hath ruffianed so upon the sea,
    What ribs of oak, when mountains melt on them,
    Can hold the mortise? What shall we hear of this?

2 GENTLEMAN A segregation of the Turkish fleet: 10
    For do but stand upon the banning shore,
    The chidden billow seems to pelt the clouds;
    The wind-shaked surge, with high and monstrous mane,
    Seems to cast water on the burning Bear
    And quench the guards of th'ever-fixèd Pole.   15
    I never did like molestation view
    On the enchafèd flood.

MONTANO   If that the Turkish fleet
    Be not ensheltered and embayed, they are drowned:
    It is impossible they bear it out.

Enter a third GENTLEMAN.

3 GENTLEMAN News, lads! Our wars are done: 20
    The desperate tempest hath so banged the Turks
    That their designment halts. A noble ship of Venice
    Hath seen a grievous wrack and sufferance
    On most part of their fleet.

MONTANO How? Is this true?

3 GENTLEMAN   The ship is here put in,   25
    A Veronesa; Michael Cassio,
    Lieutenant to the warlike Moor Othello,
    Is come on shore; the Moor himself at sea,
    And is in full commission here for Cyprus.

MONTANO I am glad on't; 'tis a worthy governor.   30

Cassio lands safely, but he is worried that Othello's ship has not yet reached shore. A messenger reports another ship is sighted and Cassio sends for news.

1 More views of Othello

Lines 1–59 contain several references to Othello. Collect them and consider what aspects of Othello the comments refer to, and whether they are generally in praise or critical of him. What group of people might the commentators be seen to represent?

2 'The Venetian Chronicle' (in small groups)

If you were a newspaper journalist reporting on the destruction of the Turkish fleet and of Othello's expected triumphant return, what kind of article would you write? Write the front page news. Your news-paper might contain news of the routing of the Turkish fleet, the storm, the fears for Othello's safety, a profile of Othello, a report on his recent marriage and interviews with witnesses/friends.

Remember, a Venetian paper would be very supportive of Othello and his exploits whereas a Cyprus-owned newspaper might view the events differently. As an alternative activity, try compiling a news-paper front page which is *not* representative of the Venetian ruling class in Cyprus.

Produce a large format front page for your classroom wall.

main sea	**allowance** reputation
th' aeriel blue sky	**surfeited to death** not excessive
indistinct regard indistinguishable	**in bold cure** healthy

3 GENTLEMAN But this same Cassio, though he speak of comfort
   Touching the Turkish loss, yet he looks sadly
   And prays the Moor be safe; for they were parted
   With foul and violent tempest.
MONTANO   Pray heaven he be;
   For I have served him, and the man commands   35
   Like a full soldier. Let's to the seaside, ho!
   As well to see the vessel that's come in
   As to throw out our eyes for brave Othello,
   Even till we make the main and th'aerial blue
   An indistinct regard.
3 GENTLEMAN   Come, let's do so;   40
   For every minute is expectancy
   Of more arrivance.

      Enter CASSIO.

CASSIO Thanks, you the valiant of this warlike isle
   That so approve the Moor. O, let the heavens
   Give him defence against the elements,   45
   For I have lost him on a dangerous sea.
MONTANO Is he well shipped?
CASSIO His bark is stoutly timbered, and his pilot
   Of very expert and approved allowance;
   Therefore my hopes, not surfeited to death,   50
   Stand in bold cure.
    [*A shout*] *within, 'A sail, a sail, a sail!'*

     Enter a MESSENGER.

CASSIO What noise?
MESSENGER The town is empty; on the brow o'the sea
   Stand ranks of people and they cry, 'A sail!'
CASSIO My hopes do shape him for the governor.   55
     A shot [*is heard within*].
2 GENTLEMAN They do discharge their shot of courtesy;
   Our friends at least.
CASSIO   I pray you, sir, go forth,
   And give us truth who 'tis that is arrived.
2 GENTLEMAN I shall.   *Exit*

Cassio describes to Montano the virtues of Desdemona. Iago is reported to have come ashore. Desdemona, Iago, Emilia and Roderigo are greeted by Cassio, but there is still no news of Othello.

1 What is your impression of Cassio? (in groups of three)

Spend about five minutes discussing how Cassio is emerging in this scene. Find quotations to support your opinions.

What advice would you give an actor playing Cassio? Go through the script in Act 2 so far and make decisions about your advice on each of Cassio's speeches.

Finally, look back at Act 1, Scene 1, lines 19–27 and Scene 3, lines 374–80 and then make a list of the qualities you think Cassio possesses. Find a photograph in a newspaper or magazine that represents 'your' Cassio.

2 'The riches of the ship' (in pairs)

This is Cassio's description of Desdemona as she comes ashore. Do you think it is exaggerated? Her father also described her as stolen treasure in Act 1. Discuss what the effect is of these two men comparing Desdemona to treasure. Do you think she would be pleased with the description?

3 Epithets

An **epithet** is an adjective or describing phrase added before a name or noun, which defines the person or thing, for example, 'valiant Othello'.

In lines 25–90 there are several examples of epithets being applied to various characters. Collect them and decide whether you think each one truly describes the named person. Are any of them applied in an ironic way?

---

paragons excels
blazoning praising
th'essential vesture the perfect
  beauty
ingener designer

enscarped drawn up into ridges
footing landing
se'nnight's week's

MONTANO But, good lieutenant, is your general wived?   60
CASSIO Most fortunately: he hath achieved a maid
        That paragons description and wild fame;
        One that excels the quirks of blazoning pens
        And in th'essential vesture of creation
        Does tire the ingener.

Enter Second Gentleman.

                    How now? Who's put in?   65
2 GENTLEMAN 'Tis one Iago, ancient to the general.
CASSIO He's had most favourable and happy speed:
        Tempests themselves, high seas, and howling winds,
        The guttered rocks and congregated sands,
        Traitors enscarped to clog the guiltless keel,   70
        As having sense of beauty do omit
        Their mortal natures, letting go safely by
        The divine Desdemona.
MONTANO   What is she?
CASSIO She that I spake of, our great captain's captain,
        Left in the conduct of the bold Iago,   75
        Whose footing here anticipates our thoughts
        A se'nnight's speed. Great Jove Othello guard
        And swell his sail with thine own powerful breath,
        That he may bless this bay with his tall ship,
        Make love's quick pants in Desdemona's arms,   80
        Give renewed fire to our extinced spirits,
        And bring all Cyprus comfort.

Enter DESDEMONA, IAGO, EMILIA *and* RODERIGO.

                     O, behold,
The riches of the ship is come on shore!
You men of Cyprus, let her have your knees.
Hail to thee, lady! And the grace of heaven,   85
Before, behind thee, and on every hand,
Enwheel thee round.
DESDEMONA   I thank you, valiant Cassio.
        What tidings can you tell me of my lord?
CASSIO He is not yet arrived; nor know I aught
        But that he's well, and will be shortly here.   90

While waiting for news of Othello's ship, Iago, Emilia and Desdemona pass the time in conversation. Iago makes provocative comments about wives and women.

1 Friendly banter or pointed comments?
(in groups of three or four)

If you were the director of the play, you would have to make a significant choice as to how to play this part of the scene. Is it light-hearted banter, the only tension being that of Desdemona awaiting news that her husband is safe? Or is there bitterness and tension arising out of Iago's pointed comments about women in general, and about his wife in particular?

Talk together about whether you think it is a scene of friendly chatter, or one tinged with misogyny (hatred of women) and domestic strife.

Read the page of script through in different ways and try to decide which sounds best.

2 The kiss

When Cassio kisses Emilia, he apologises first to Iago for his 'bold show of courtesy' and puts it down to his good 'breeding' and 'manners'. How would *you* interpret Cassio's behaviour?

- he's a macho flirt with a reputation to keep up
- he's a naturally courteous man
- he's deliberately winding Iago up
- he's aware of Iago's jealous nature
- he's trying to be nice to everyone at a difficult moment
- he's not very confident in social situations
- he's deliberately patronising Emilia
- some other interpretation.

Decide how you would like Iago to react.

---

have list want
pictures silent

bells noisy
assay try

DESDEMONA O, but I fear – how lost you company?

CASSIO The great contention of the sea and skies
    Parted our fellowship.
        [*A shout*] *within, 'A sail, a sail!'* [*A shot is heard.*]
        But hark, a sail!

2 GENTLEMAN They give their greeting to the citadel:
    This likewise is a friend.

CASSIO   See for the news.   95
                   [*Exit Second Gentleman*]
    Good ancient, you are welcome. [*To Emilia*] Welcome,
      mistress.
    Let it not gall your patience, good Iago,
    That I extend my manners. 'Tis my breeding
    That gives me this bold show of courtesy.
            [*He kisses Emilia.*]

IAGO Sir, would she give you so much of her lips   100
    As of her tongue she oft bestows on me
    You would have enough.

DESDEMONA Alas, she has no speech.

IAGO   In faith, too much:
    I find it still when I have list to sleep.
    Marry, before your ladyship, I grant   105
    She puts her tongue a little in her heart
    And chides with thinking.

EMILIA   You've little cause to say so.

IAGO Come on, come on; you are pictures out of doors, bells in
    your parlours, wild-cats in your kitchens, saints in your injuries,
    devils being offended, players in your housewifery, and   110
    housewives in your beds.

DESDEMONA O fie upon thee, slanderer!

IAGO Nay, it is true, or else I am a Turk:
    You rise to play and go to bed to work.

EMILIA You shall not write my praise.

IAGO   No, let me not.   115

DESDEMONA What wouldst thou write of me, if thou shouldst
    praise me?

IAGO O, gentle lady, do not put me to't,
    For I am nothing if not critical.

DESDEMONA Come on, assay. There's one gone to the harbour?

IAGO Ay, madam.   120

Desdemona reveals she is deliberately joining in the conversation to take her mind off waiting for Othello. Iago continues to joke about women.

1 Playing with language (in pairs)

Theatre-going Elizabethans were amused and fascinated by all types of language and language play. **Epigrams** were very popular in Elizabethan drama. An epigram is a concise, witty poem which often ends on a surprising turn of thought. Sardonic generalisations were commonly put into the mouths of down-to-earth 'honest' characters.

Talk together about what Iago's comments opposite reveal about him.

2 Connotations and puns

The words 'fair' and 'black' are used repeatedly in this play. Not only are they used to denote the actual physical colouring of Othello and Desdemona, but they also carry certain connotative meanings (associations), which Iago in particular is keen to exploit.

How many meanings can you come up with for the words 'fair' and 'black'? Look back at the Duke's use of the two words in Act 1, Scene 3, lines 285–6.

Puns (where words sound the same but have quite different meanings) were a highly fashionable form of word play in Elizabethan drama. In *Romeo and Juliet*, Mercutio has been fatally stabbed and yet he makes a pun: 'ask for me tomorrow and you shall find me a grave man . . .'.

Iago puns on the word 'white':

What other puns can you find in Iago's speeches opposite?

birdlime sticky substance to catch birds
frieze woollen cloth
muse goddess of poetry

DESDEMONA [*Aside*] I am not merry, but I do beguile
    The thing I am by seeming otherwise –
    Come, how wouldst thou praise me?
IAGO I am about it, but indeed my invention
    Comes from my pate as birdlime does from frieze –   125
    It plucks out brains and all. But my muse labours,
    And thus she is delivered:
    'If she be fair and wise, fairness and wit,
    The one's for use, the other useth it.'
DESDEMONA Well praised! How if she be black and witty?   130
IAGO 'If she be black, and thereto have a wit,
    She'll find a white that shall her blackness fit.'
DESDEMONA Worse and worse.
EMILIA   How if fair and foolish?
IAGO 'She never yet was foolish that was fair,
    For even her folly helped her to an heir.'   135
DESDEMONA These are old fond paradoxes to make fools laugh
    i'th'alehouse. What miserable praise hast thou for her that's foul
    and foolish?
IAGO 'There's none so foul and foolish thereunto,
    But does foul pranks which fair and wise ones do.'   140
DESDEMONA O heavy ignorance! Thou praisest the worst best. But
    what praise couldst thou bestow on a deserving woman indeed? One
    that in the authority of her merit did justly put on the vouch of
    very malice itself?
IAGO 'She that was ever fair, and never proud,   145
    Had tongue at will, and yet was never loud;
    Never lacked gold, and yet went never gay;
    Fled from her wish, and yet said "Now I may";
    She that being angered, her revenge being nigh,
    Bade her wrong stay, and her displeasure fly;   150
    She that in wisdom never was so frail
    To change the cod's head for the salmon's tail;
    She that could think and ne'er disclose her mind,
    See suitors following and not look behind;
    She was a wight, if ever such wight were –'   155
DESDEMONA To do what?
IAGO 'To suckle fools and chronicle small beer.'
DESDEMONA O, most lame and impotent conclusion! Do not learn of
    him, Emilia, though he be thy husband. How say you, Cassio, is
    he not a most profane and liberal counsellor?   160

Othello

> *Iago revels in Cassio's attention to Desdemona, seeing in it a way in which he can ruin Cassio. Othello arrives safely. He and Desdemona greet each other, speaking of happiness and love.*

1 'An excellent courtesy!' (in groups of three or four)

Read Iago's aside to the audience (lines 163–71) and then act it out, matching the movements of Cassio and Desdemona to Iago's commentary. Where should Iago stand, and how should he say the words? Iago uses several images in his speech, in turn: a spider's web, a snare ('gyve') and, lastly, tubes for inserting enemas into the rectum ('clyster-pipes')!

If you have enough people in your group you could also include either Roderigo or Emilia, and show what they might be engaged in at this point.

2 Greetings (in pairs)

Read lines 174–91 and decide on what you agree to be the *key* word in each line. Devise a presentation of these selected words. Keeping them in the right order. Show it to the rest of the class.

3 Another kiss (in small groups)

Spend about five minutes discussing how you would differentiate between the three different kisses contained in this scene so far. You could show them in frozen picture form and get the rest of the class to identify each . . . It is a fascinating exercise to include Iago's different reaction to each one.

home plainly
bark ship

Olympus mountain home of the gods in classical mythology
if it were now to die if I were to die now

CASSIO He speaks home, madam; you may relish him more in the
soldier than in the scholar.

IAGO [*Aside*] He takes her by the palm. Ay, well said; whisper.
With as little a web as this will I ensnare as great a fly as Cassio.
Ay, smile upon her, do. I will gyve thee in thine own courtship.   165
You say true, 'tis so indeed. If such tricks as these strip you out
of your lieutenantry, it had been better you had not kissed your
three fingers so oft, which now again you are most apt to play the
sir in. Very good, well kissed, an excellent courtesy! 'Tis so
indeed. Yet again your fingers to your lips? Would they were   170
clyster-pipes for your sake!

Trumpets within.

The Moor! I know his trumpet.

CASSIO   'Tis truly so.

DESDEMONA Let's meet him and receive him.

CASSIO   Lo, where he comes!

Enter OTHELLO *and* ATTENDANTS.

OTHELLO O, my fair warrior!

DESDEMONA   My dear Othello!

OTHELLO It gives me wonder great as my content   175
To see you here before me. O, my soul's joy,
If after every tempest come such calms,
May the winds blow till they have wakened death,
And let the labouring bark climb hills of seas,
Olympus-high, and duck again as low   180
As hell's from heaven. If it were now to die,
'Twere now to be most happy; for I fear
My soul hath her content so absolute
That not another comfort like to this
Succeeds in unknown fate.

DESDEMONA   The heavens forbid   185
But that our loves and comforts should increase,
Even as our days do grow.

OTHELLO   Amen to that, sweet powers!
I cannot speak enough of this content;
It stops me here; it is too much of joy.

They kiss.

And this, and this, the greatest discords be   190
That e'er our hearts shall make.

*Othello and Desdemona go off together, leaving Iago alone with Roderigo.
Iago tells him that Desdemona is in love with Cassio, because she must
necessarily tire of Othello.*

1 Making sweet music together

Iago's comment (line 191) that Othello and his wife 'are well tuned' is
followed by his vow 'to set down the pegs' (to slacken the strings of an
instrument). The metaphor uses the harmony of music to indicate the
current harmony of Othello's marriage, and Iago's intention to
disrupt that harmony.

(For an activity on metaphors, see page 90.)

2 Othello's voyage

Write Othello's ship's log for his journey to Cyprus. You might
include some of the following:

- thoughts on setting out
- plans to defend Cyprus
- early encounters with the Turkish ships
- thoughts about Desdemona
- a description of the storm
- fears for Desdemona's safety
- feelings on reaching harbour safely.

3 Iago's argument (in pairs)

According to Iago, Othello is defective in 'loveliness in favour,
sympathy in years, manners and beauties . . .'. He assures Roderigo
that Desdemona will quickly tire of her husband 'when the blood is
made dull with the act of sport . . .' and that she had only been
attracted to his 'bragging' and 'fantastical lies'.

Read lines 212–35 to each other, taking turns to read small
sections.

On what evidence is Iago basing his version of Othello and
Desdemona's relationship? How convincing a case does Iago manage
to put together for Roderigo's sake?

I dote I'm not making sense
master captain of the ship
list me listen to me

lay thy finger thus put your finger
  to your lips (ssshh!)
compassing achieving
salt lecherous

IAGO [*Aside*]   O, you are well tuned now!
But I'll set down the pegs that make this music,
As honest as I am.

OTHELLO   Come, let us to the castle.
News, friends; our wars are done; the Turks are drowned.
How does my old acquaintance of this isle?   195
Honey, you shall be well desired in Cyprus;
I have found great love amongst them. O my sweet,
I prattle out of fashion and I dote
In mine own comforts. I prithee, good Iago,
Go to the bay and disembark my coffers;   200
Bring thou the master to the citadel;
He is a good one, and his worthiness
Does challenge much respect. Come, Desdemona,
Once more well met at Cyprus!

Exeunt [*all except Iago and Roderigo*]

IAGO [*To a departing Attendant*] Do thou meet me presently at the   205
harbour. [*To Roderigo*] Come hither. If thou be'st valiant – as
they say base men being in love have then a nobility in their
natures more than is native to them – list me. The lieutenant
tonight watches on the court of guard. First, I must tell thee this:
Desdemona is directly in love with him.   210

RODERIGO With him? Why, 'tis not possible!

IAGO Lay thy finger thus, and let thy soul be instructed. Mark me
with what violence she first loved the Moor but for bragging and
telling her fantastical lies. And will she love him still for prating?
Let not thy discreet heart think it. Her eye must be fed. And   215
what delight shall she have to look on the devil? When the blood
is made dull with the act of sport, there should be, again to
inflame it and to give satiety a fresh appetite, loveliness in
favour, sympathy in years, manners and beauties: all which the
Moor is defective in. Now for want of these required conveniences,   220
her delicate tenderness will find itself abused, begin to heave the
gorge, disrelish and abhor the Moor. Very nature will instruct
her in it, and compel her to some second choice. Now, sir, this
granted – as it is a most pregnant and unforced position – who
stands so eminent in the degree of this fortune as Cassio does? – a   225
knave very voluble; no further conscionable than in putting on
the mere form of civil and humane seeming for the better
compassing of his salt and most hidden loose affection.

Iago assures Roderigo that Desdemona has tired of Othello, and has her eye on other men. Iago tells his plan. He urges Roderigo to provoke Cassio to anger that night. The resulting riot will ruin Cassio's prospects.

1 'A slipper and subtle knave' (in pairs)

Read Iago's description of Cassio (lines 229–34). Pick out any points which you agree to be an accurate portrait of Cassio.

Which character would the remaining description fit best?

2 The provocation? (in pairs)

Iago's plot to provoke Cassio into a fight with Roderigo is in lines 248–62. From what you know of both characters, improvise the situation. What comments might Roderigo make to aggravate Cassio?

3 A romantic image

Iago says of Cassio and Desdemona: 'They met so near with their lips that their breaths embraced together . . .'

Coming from Iago, this is scornful (and a distortion of the truth!). But in another situation it would be a highly romantic image. Either make a design based on the words, or write a paragraph or two in the genre of a love story, ending with the quotation.

4 An anti-romantic image! (in pairs)

Have you ever felt annoyed at friends idealising someone they admire to an impossible extent? If so, you probably enjoyed reading Iago's terse retort to Roderigo's protestation about Desdemona's state of blessedness:

'Blest fig's end! The wine she drinks is made of grapes.'

Invent other such down-to-earth comments for people liable to be treated as being somehow above mere mortals.

---

slipper slippery
stamp and counterfeit make a
  forgery of
fig's end rubbish

in choler when angry
qualification pacifying

Why none; why none – a slipper and subtle knave, a finder
out of occasions, that has an eye can stamp and counterfeit   230
advantages, though true advantage never present itself; a
devilish knave! Besides, the knave is handsome, young, and hath
all those requisites in him that folly and green minds look after.
A pestilent complete knave; and the woman hath found him
already.   235

RODERIGO I cannot believe that in her; she's full of most blest
condition.

IAGO Blest fig's end! The wine she drinks is made of grapes. If she
had been blest she would never have loved the Moor. Blest
pudding! Didst thou not see her paddle with the palm of his   240
hand? Didst not mark that?

RODERIGO Yes, that I did; but that was but courtesy.

IAGO Lechery, by this hand: an index and obscure prologue to the
history of lust and foul thoughts. They met so near with their lips
that their breaths embraced together – villainous thoughts,   245
Roderigo! When these mutualities so marshal the way, hard
at hand comes the master and main exercise, the incorporate
conclusion. Pish! But, sir, be you ruled by me. I have brought
you from Venice; watch you tonight; for the command, I'll lay't
upon you. Cassio knows you not; I'll not be far from you. Do you   250
find some occasion to anger Cassio, either by speaking too loud or
tainting his discipline, or from what other course you please,
which the time shall more favourably minister.

RODERIGO Well.

IAGO Sir, he's rash and very sudden in choler, and haply with his   255
truncheon may strike at you: provoke him that he may; for even
out of that will I cause these of Cyprus to mutiny, whose
qualification shall come into no true taste again but by the
displanting of Cassio. So shall you have a shorter journey to your
desires by the means I shall then have to prefer them, and the   260
impediment most profitably removed without the which there
were no expectation of our prosperity.

RODERIGO I will do this, if you can bring it to any opportunity.

IAGO I warrant thee. Meet me by and by at the citadel. I must fetch
his necessaries ashore. Farewell.   265

RODERIGO Adieu.   *Exit*

Iago again says that he is seeking revenge because he suspects that Othello has slept with Emilia. He plans to use Roderigo to ensure the downfall of Cassio, whom he also suspects has made love to Emilia.

1 The psychiatrist's couch (in pairs)

Imagine Iago is being questioned by a psychiatrist about his obsession with Othello and Cassio. Work out what questions you would want to ask Iago, and use lines from the soliloquy opposite to provide Iago's answers. Improvise the scene.

Frank Finlay as Iago, National Theatre, 1964.

howbeit even though	**trace** follow after (hunting term)
peradventure perhaps	**on the hip** at my mercy (hunting
accountant accountable	metaphor)
leaped into my seat made love to	**rank garb** foul manner
my wife	**with my night-cap** in my bed
inwards innards, guts	**egregiously** extraordinarily,
	outstandingly
	practising upon plotting against

IAGO That Cassio loves her, I do well believe't;
That she loves him, 'tis apt and of great credit.
The Moor, howbeit that I endure him not,
Is of a constant, loving, noble nature;   270
And I dare think he'll prove to Desdemona
A most dear husband. Now, I do love her too,
Not out of absolute lust – though peradventure
I stand accountant for as great a sin –
But partly led to diet my revenge,   275
For that I do suspect the lusty Moor
Hath leaped into my seat, the thought whereof
Doth like a poisonous mineral gnaw my inwards;
And nothing can or shall content my soul
Till I am evened with him, wife for wife;   280
Or failing so, yet that I put the Moor
At least into a jealousy so strong
That judgement cannot cure. Which thing to do,
If this poor trash of Venice, whom I trace
For his quick hunting, stand the putting on,   285
I'll have our Michael Cassio on the hip,
Abuse him to the Moor in the rank garb –
For I fear Cassio with my night-cap too –
Make the Moor thank me, love me, and reward me,
For making him egregiously an ass,   290
And practising upon his peace and quiet
Even to madness. 'Tis here, but yet confused;
Knavery's plain face is never seen till used.   *Exit*

65

A Herald publicly announces celebrations to mark the destruction of the Turkish fleet. They also honour Othello's wedding. Scene 3 opens with Othello bidding Cassio to inspect the guard at night.

1 The proclamation (in pairs)

Read the Herald's proclamation aloud. If you were directing the play would you cut this or keep it in? Give your reasons.

Decide how the scene ought to be performed: straight to the audience, spoken to a crowd on stage, with the Herald mingling in the audience, or some other dramatically effective way.

2 Another point of view (in groups of three or four)

Imagine three or four ordinary Cypriot field workers pausing from their labours to listen to the proclamation. Improvise *their* particular reaction to each section of it.

3 'Iago is most honest'

This fairly obvious piece of dramatic irony comes almost immediately after Iago's vow to drive Othello 'even to madness'. What effect do you think Othello's comment would have on an audience in the theatre?

If this were a pantomime, such a misguided comment by the hero would invite the audience to shout out to warn him! Write down what you would want to say to Othello at this moment, if you had the chance to step out of the audience onto the stage with the characters!

---

mere perdition total destruction
offices kitchens, food stores

full liberty free
out-sport discretion celebrate to excess

ACT 2 SCENE 2
Cyprus A street

Enter Othello's HERALD *with a proclamation*

HERALD It is Othello's pleasure, our noble and valiant general, that
upon certain tidings now arrived importing the mere perdition
of the Turkish fleet, every man put himself into triumph: some
to dance, some to make bonfires, each man to what sport and revels
his addiction leads him; for besides these beneficial news, it is   5
the celebration of his nuptial. So much was his pleasure should
be proclaimed. All offices are open, and there is full liberty of
feasting from this present hour of five till the bell have told
eleven. Heaven bless the isle of Cyprus and our noble general
Othello!   *Exit*   10

ACT 2 SCENE 3
Cyprus A room in the castle

Enter OTHELLO, DESDEMONA, CASSIO *and* ATTENDANTS

OTHELLO Good Michael, look you to the guard tonight.
  Let's teach ourselves that honourable stop,
  Not to out-sport discretion.
CASSIO Iago hath direction what to do;
  But notwithstanding with my personal eye   5
  Will I look to't.
OTHELLO   Iago is most honest.
  Michael, good night; tomorrow with your earliest
  Let me have speech with you – Come, my dear love,
  The purchase made, the fruits are to ensue;
  That profit's yet to come 'tween me and you.   10
  Good night.
              Exeunt Othello, Desdemona [and Attendants]

Iago persuades Cassio to join in the celebrations with various male friends. Cassio reveals he has a poor head for alcohol, and declines to drink further. Iago plans to make Cassio drunk and quarrelsome.

1 Typical men? (in pairs)

Read the dialogue between Iago and Cassio. Consider whether it conforms to your expectations of male 'barrack-room' conversation that soldiers have in their living quarters. What differences can you detect between the two speakers in their attitudes?

Act out the dialogue up to line 39 in such a way as to highlight any significant differences between the two men and the nature of their remarks. For fun, you could exaggerate it to the point of parody!

2 Iago's plan (in groups of four)

Read through Iago's soliloquy (lines 40–55), taking turns to read up to each full stop. Now reduce the information contained within each sentence to a key phrase or group of words. Present your abbreviated version of the soliloquy to the rest of the class.

---

cast dismissed
Jove King of the Gods, known for his sexual prowess
game sexual tricks
parley summons, invitation

stoup jug
craftily qualified carefully diluted
potations pottle-deep many mugs or tankards of drink

Enter IAGO.

CASSIO Welcome, Iago; we must to the watch.

IAGO Not this hour, lieutenant; 'tis not yet ten o'th'clock. Our general cast us thus early for the love of his Desdemona; who let us not therefore blame: he hath not yet made wanton the night with her, and she is sport for Jove.   15

CASSIO She's a most exquisite lady.

IAGO And I'll warrant her full of game.

CASSIO Indeed she is a most fresh and delicate creature.

IAGO What an eye she has! Methinks it sounds a parley to provocation.   20

CASSIO An inviting eye, and yet methinks right modest.

IAGO And when she speaks, is it not an alarum to love?

CASSIO She is indeed perfection.

IAGO Well, happiness to their sheets! Come, lieutenant, I have a stoup of wine, and here without are a brace of Cyprus gallants, that would fain have a measure to the health of the black Othello.   25

CASSIO Not tonight, good Iago; I have very poor and unhappy brains for drinking. I could well wish courtesy would invent some other custom of entertainment.   30

IAGO O, they are our friends – but one cup; I'll drink for you.

CASSIO I have drunk but one cup tonight, and that was craftily qualified too; and behold what innovation it makes here. I am unfortunate in the infirmity and dare not task my weakness with any more.   35

IAGO What, man! 'Tis a night of revels; the gallants desire it.

CASSIO Where are they?

IAGO Here at the door; I pray you call them in.

CASSIO I'll do't, but it dislikes me.   *Exit*

IAGO If I can fasten but one cup upon him,   40
    With that which he hath drunk tonight already,
    He'll be as full of quarrel and offence
    As my young mistress' dog. Now my sick fool Roderigo,
    Whom love hath turned almost the wrong side out,
    To Desdemona hath tonight caroused   45
    Potations pottle-deep, and he's to watch.

Iago gets the party going, singing drinking songs.

---

1 'My boat sails freely' (in pairs)

Iago's metaphor:

'My boat sails freely, both with wind and stream' (line 55)

echoes earlier imagery. Work out what Iago means by this image and talk together about whether you think it is appropriate, and why.

2 Times don't change! (in groups of four or five)

As one student wrote in an essay, 'this scene could be taking place in any number of pubs around Britain today, with its all male rowdiness, drinking songs (could be football/rugby songs?) and comments on the comparative drinking prowess of different nationalities . . .'.

Do you agree with her view of lines 56–74?

3 Iago (the whole class)

Iago is a man of many parts. Here he is demonstrating a sociable side, someone who is fun to be with. Discuss what other parts or roles Iago has played so far.

---

that hold their honours in a wary distance quick to protect their honour
flustered confused
rouse drink

cannikin drinking can, tankard
potent in potting heavy drinkers
Almain German

Three lads of Cyprus, noble swelling spirits,
That hold their honours in a wary distance,
The very elements of this warlike isle,
Have I tonight flustered with flowing cups;   50
And they watch too. Now, 'mongst this flock of
      drunkards,
Am I to put our Cassio in some action
That may offend the isle. But here they come.

Enter Cassio, MONTANO *and* GENTLEMEN.

If consequence do but approve my dream,
My boat sails freely, both with wind and stream.   55
CASSIO 'Fore God, they have given me a rouse already.
MONTANO Good faith, a little one; not past a pint, as I am a soldier.
IAGO Some wine, ho!
      [*Sings*]
      And let me the cannikin clink, clink,
      And let me the cannikin clink;   60
         A soldier's a man,
         O, man's life's but a span,
      Why then, let a soldier drink.
   Some wine, boys!
CASSIO 'Fore God, an excellent song.   65
IAGO I learned it in England, where indeed they are most potent in
      potting. Your Dane, your German, and your swag-bellied
      Hollander – drink, ho! – are nothing to your English.
CASSIO Is your Englishman so exquisite in his drinking?
IAGO Why, he drinks you with facility your Dane dead drunk; he sweats   70
      not to overthrow your Almain; he gives your Hollander a vomit
      ere the next pottle can be filled.
CASSIO To the health of our general!
MONTANO I am for it, lieutenant, and I'll do you justice.

The party continues and Cassio becomes drunk very quickly. Cassio goes off to take his turn on guard, and Iago comments on his dangerous 'vice': his weakness for alcohol.

1 Party photograph (in groups of four to six)

Take line 97 'Do not think, gentlemen, I am drunk' and imagine freezing the action on stage. Create this photograph or freeze-frame, each person making it clear from the way they are positioned who they represent.

The rest of the class guess the characters in each photograph.

2 The drunk (in pairs)

Acting a drunk is one of the most difficult tasks for any actor. But in lines 85–121, Shakespeare provides a script for Cassio that really does catch the rhythms of drunken speech. Take parts and read the lines using any actions you think appropriate. Experiment!

3 The drinking song

Iago sings two verses of a rousing drinking song, 'King Stephen was and a worthy peer . . .' (lines 76–83). Exactly imitating the rhythm and the rhyme pattern, compose an appropriate third verse. If you can, find a tune to fit the words and then accompany yourself and others in your class.

---

lown rogue
wight man
degree status
platform gun ramparts

set the watch mount the guard
just equinox exact equivalent or
  counterbalance

IAGO O sweet England!   75

  [*Sings*]

  King Stephen was and a worthy peer,
    His breeches cost him but a crown;
  He held them sixpence all too dear,
    With that he called the tailor lown.

  He was a wight of high renown,   80
    And thou art but of low degree;
  'Tis pride that pulls the country down;
    Then take thine auld cloak about thee.

  Some wine, ho!

CASSIO 'Fore God, this is a more exquisite song than the other.   85

IAGO Will you hear't again?

CASSIO No, for I hold him to be unworthy of his place that does those things. Well, God's above all, and there be souls must be saved, and there be souls must not be saved.

IAGO It's true, good lieutenant.   90

CASSIO For mine own part – no offence to the general, nor any man of quality – I hope to be saved.

IAGO And so do I too, lieutenant.

CASSIO Ay, but by your leave, not before me; the lieutenant is to be saved before the ancient. Let's have no more of this; let's to our   95 affairs. God forgive us our sins! Gentlemen, let's look to our business. Do not think, gentlemen, I am drunk; this is my ancient, this is my right hand, and this is my left hand. I am not drunk now, I can stand well enough, and I speak well enough.

ALL Excellent well.   100

CASSIO Why, very well then; you must not think then that I am drunk.   *Exit*

MONTANO To the platform, masters. Come, let's set the watch.

IAGO You see this fellow that is gone before,
  He is a soldier fit to stand by Caesar   105
  And give direction. And do but see his vice –
  'Tis to his virtue a just equinox,
  The one as long as th'other. 'Tis pity of him.
  I fear the trust Othello puts him in,
  On some odd time of his infirmity,   110
  Will shake this island.

Montano thinks that Othello should be told of Cassio's weakness for drink. Iago sends Roderigo after Cassio, and the two re-enter fighting. Montano tries to stop Cassio striking Roderigo.

1 An honest action (in small groups)

Iago is constantly associated with the word 'honest' in the play. Discuss how appropriate you think this is, and what effect it might have on an audience. Flick back through the play so far and find any other moments where 'honest' has been applied to Iago. Jot down the line references and the speakers, then compare your findings with those of other groups.

2 What did Roderigo do? (in pairs)

So, what happened outside? What *did* Roderigo do or say to annoy Cassio so much? Take line 130 as a clue, then improvise the incident.

horologe a double set twice round the clock
put in mind told
hazard risk

ingraft deep-rooted
twiggen bottle bottle encased in wicker-work
mazzard head, skull

MONTANO   But is he often thus?

IAGO 'Tis evermore the prologue to his sleep:
       He'll watch the horologe a double set,
       If drink rock not his cradle.

MONTANO   It were well
       The general were put in mind of it.   115
       Perhaps he sees it not, or his good nature
       Prizes the virtue that appears in Cassio
       And looks not on his evils: is not this true?

                 Enter RODERIGO.

IAGO [*Aside to Roderigo*] How now, Roderigo?
       I pray you after the lieutenant, go.   120

                                      Exit Roderigo

MONTANO And 'tis great pity that the noble Moor
       Should hazard such a place as his own second
       With one of an ingraft infirmity;
       It were an honest action to say so
       To the Moor.

IAGO   Not I, for this fair island: 125
       I do love Cassio well, and would do much
       To cure him of this evil.
                 [*A cry of*] '*Help, help!*' *within.*
                      But hark! what noise?

                 Enter Cassio, pursuing Roderigo.

CASSIO Zounds, you rogue, you rascal!
MONTANO What's the matter, lieutenant?
CASSIO A knave teach me my duty! I'll beat the knave into a   130
       twiggen bottle.
RODERIGO Beat me?
CASSIO Dost thou prate, rogue?
                 [*He strikes Roderigo.*]
MONTANO Nay, good lieutenant, I pray you, sir, hold your hand.
CASSIO Let me go, sir; or I'll knock you o'er the mazzard.   135
MONTANO Come, come, you're drunk.

Cassio, incensed by Montano's accusation of drunkenness, fights him. The alarm is sounded. Othello enters to restore order and demand an explanation. Iago denies he knows who began the brawl.

1 The fight (in groups of five or six)

Create a slow motion, silent version of the scene from line 128, 'Enter Cassio pursuing Roderigo . . .' to line 150, 'From whence ariseth this?'. Make each character visibly recognisable and each stage of the action clearly defined. Remember: slow motion, safety, and clarity of action are your guides.

2 Honest Iago (in pairs)

There's that description again (line 158)! Take a large sheet of paper and design a graphic presentation of all the uses of 'honest' in the script so far.

Leave room for further additions to the list – you'll find that examples come thick and fast in the rest of this scene. Add to your diagram as you read the rest of the play.

Example:

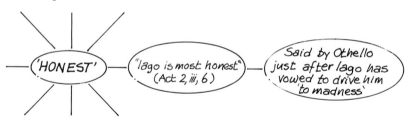

3 Iago's language

Iago chooses his words to suit his listeners. In lines 160–8, find three or four expressions that Iago knows will appeal to Othello. Give reasons for your choice.

Diabolo the devil
rise riot
carve for his own rage stab
  someone in anger

holds his soul light doesn't value
  his life
quarter friendship

CASSIO Drunk?

They fight.

IAGO [*Aside to Roderigo*] Away I say, go out and cry a mutiny.

[*Exit Roderigo*]

    Nay, good lieutenant; God's will, gentlemen!
    Help ho! Lieutenant, sir! Montano, sir!   140
    Help, masters, here's a goodly watch indeed!

A bell rings.

    Who's that which rings the bell? Diabolo, ho!
    The town will rise. God's will, lieutenant, hold!
    You will be shamed forever.

Enter Othello, and GENTLEMEN *with weapons.*

OTHELLO What is the matter here?

MONTANO   Zounds, I bleed still.   145
    I am hurt to th'death.

OTHELLO   Hold for your lives!

IAGO Hold ho, lieutenant, sir; Montano, gentlemen,
    Have you forgot all place of sense and duty?
    Hold! the general speaks to you; hold, for shame!

OTHELLO Why, how now, ho! From whence ariseth this?   150
    Are we turned Turks, and to ourselves do that
    Which heaven hath forbid the Ottomites?
    For Christian shame, put by this barbarous brawl.
    He that stirs next to carve for his own rage
    Holds his soul light: he dies upon his motion.   155
    Silence that dreadful bell: it frights the isle
    From her propriety. What is the matter, masters?
    Honest Iago, that looks dead with grieving,
    Speak. Who began this? On thy love, I charge thee.

IAGO I do not know. Friends all but now, even now,   160
    In quarter and in terms like bride and groom,
    Divesting them for bed; and then but now –
    As if some planet had unwitted men –
    Swords out and tilting one at other's breasts
    In opposition bloody. I cannot speak   165
    Any beginning to this peevish odds:
    And would in action glorious I had lost
    Those legs that brought me to a part of it.

Othello tries to discover who started the fight. Cassio gives no explanation.
Montano pleads self-defence, and says Iago knows as much as he does.
Othello orders Iago to speak.

1 Cassio (in pairs)

When questioned, Cassio chooses to say nothing. Do you think that is the right course of action? If not, what *should* he have said? Spend about five minutes creating a possible reply for Cassio.

2 Why is Othello so angry? (in small groups)

Go back over the scene from the point of Othello's entrance to line 198. Suggest at least four factors that contribute to Othello's rage: why his 'passion . . . Assays to lead the way'.

3 'Collied'

Othello indicates that he is on the verge of losing his temper with the brawlers. At line 187 he exclaims:

'. . . passion having my best judgement collied,
Assays to lead the way.'

He is saying that his passion or rage is about to take over from his better ('best') judgement. The word 'collied' is usually defined as 'blackened', with its links with the word 'coal' ('collier', 'colliery'). What do you think is meant by 'collied' here? What other associations might it carry?

---

censure judgement
self-charity self-defence
assays attempts

partially affined taking sides
leagued in office intimidated by
  being of inferior rank

OTHELLO How comes it, Michael, you are thus forgot?

CASSIO I pray you pardon me, I cannot speak.   170

OTHELLO Worthy Montano, you were wont be civil:
        The gravity and stillness of your youth
        The world hath noted; and your name is great
        In mouths of wisest censure. What's the matter
        That you unlace your reputation thus,   175
        And spend your rich opinion for the name
        Of a night-brawler? Give me answer to it.

MONTANO Worthy Othello, I am hurt to danger;
        Your officer Iago can inform you –
        While I spare speech, which something now offends me –   180
        Of all that I do know; nor know I aught
        By me that's said or done amiss this night,
        Unless self-charity be sometimes a vice,
        And to defend ourselves it be a sin
        When violence assails us.

OTHELLO   Now by heaven   185
        My blood begins my safer guides to rule,
        And passion having my best judgement collied,
        Assays to lead the way. Zounds, if I stir,
        Or do but lift this arm, the best of you
        Shall sink in my rebuke. Give me to know   190
        How this foul rout began, who set it on,
        And he that is approved in this offence,
        Though he had twinned with me, both at a birth,
        Shall lose me. What, in a town of war,
        Yet wild, the people's hearts brimful of fear,   195
        To manage private and domestic quarrel,
        In night, and on the court and guard of safety?
        'Tis monstrous. Iago, who began't?

MONTANO If partially affined or leagued in office,
        Thou dost deliver more or less than truth,   200
        Thou art no soldier.

IAGO   Touch me not so near.
        I had rather have this tongue cut from my mouth
        Than it should do offence to Michael Cassio.

Iago gives an account of how Cassio started the affray. Saying Iago's honesty has made him play down Cassio's offence, Othello immediately dismisses Cassio from office.

1 Gossip column (in pairs)

Write an account of the barrack-room party and its outcome, as if for the gossip column of the local *Cyprus Mail*. Whose version of events might be reflected and what other gossip might be contained in the column? Remember, gossip columnists also make all sorts of general comments about people's personalities.

2 Iago's diary

Consider how well Iago has orchestrated the whole incident of the brawl. Do you think Iago would feel pleased with the way he has played his part as a loyal friend to Cassio, yet obliged to tell the truth to his commanding officer, Othello?

Write Iago's diary entry for that day's events. Pay attention to the kind of language he is likely to use, and try to incorporate quotations where possible in your account. Have Iago think back over all he said to Othello in lines 201–27, and commenting on his own words. At the end, indicate how successfully Iago considers he has set things up for his future plans.

3 Headlines – what's happened so far?

There are three scenes in Act 1 and three scenes in Act 2. Imagine you are a newspaper sub-editor. Decide what type of paper you work for ('serious' or 'popular'). Your job is to write brief, memorable headlines for each of the six scenes so far. Make your headlines as accurate as possible, but remember, they must be short.

---

fall in fright become alarmed
I returned . . . that I thought it
  best to turn back because

indignity insult
mince this matter tone it down

Yet, I persuade myself, to speak the truth
Shall nothing wrong him. This it is, general: 205
Montano and myself being in speech,
There comes a fellow crying out for help,
And Cassio following him with determined sword
To execute upon him. Sir, this gentleman
Steps in to Cassio and entreats his pause;   210
Myself the crying fellow did pursue,
Lest by his clamour – as it so fell out –
The town might fall in fright. He, swift of foot,
Outran my purpose and I returned the rather
For that I heard the clink and fall of swords   215
And Cassio high in oath, which till tonight
I ne'er might say before. When I came back –
For this was brief – I found them close together
At blow and thrust, even as again they were
When you yourself did part them.   220
More of this matter can I not report;
But men are men; the best sometimes forget.
Though Cassio did some little wrong to him,
As men in rage strike those that wish them best,
Yet surely Cassio, I believe, received   225
From him that fled some strange indignity
Which patience could not pass.
OTHELLO   I know, Iago,
Thy honesty and love doth mince this matter,
Making it light to Cassio. Cassio, I love thee,
But never more be officer of mine.   230

Enter Desdemona attended.

Look if my gentle love be not raised up!
I'll make thee an example.
DESDEMONA   What's the matter, dear?
OTHELLO All's well now, sweeting; come away to bed.
Sir, for your hurts myself will be your surgeon.
                              [*Montano is led off*]

After Othello has gone back to bed, Cassio bemoans the loss of his reputation to Iago. Iago tells him to make an appeal. Cassio curses what drink does to men.

1 Reputation (in pairs)

Read lines 242–9 to each other several times. Cassio defines reputation as:

'the immortal part of myself', without which, 'what remains is bestial'.

In contrast, Iago defines reputation as:

'an idle and most false imposition, oft got without merit and lost without deserving'.

Talk together and make notes, outlining how far you consider these two conflicting definitions to have significance for each of the two speakers.

2 Campaign against alcohol (in groups of three or four)

Imagine that Cassio has been employed by the Venetian Health Education Council to make a series of advertisements outlining the dangers of alcohol abuse.

Design the campaign, complete with a suitable logo, a slogan (taken from the script, if possible) and other gimmicks. Improvise a three minute television commercial featuring Cassio's account of his own personal experiences at the hands of the 'invisible spirit of wine'.

---

cast in his mood dismissed in anger
sue appeal

fustian rubbish, bombastic nonsense
nothing wherefore not what it was about

Iago, look with care about the town,   235
And silence those whom this vile brawl distracted.
Come, Desdemona, 'tis the soldier's life
To have their balmy slumbers waked with strife.

Exeunt [all but Iago and Cassio]

IAGO What, are you hurt, lieutenant?

CASSIO Ay, past all surgery.   240

IAGO Marry, God forbid!

CASSIO Reputation, reputation, reputation! O, I have lost my
reputation! I have lost the immortal part of myself, and what
remains is bestial. My reputation, Iago, my reputation!

IAGO As I am an honest man, I thought you had received some bodily   245
wound: there is more of sense in that than in reputation.
Reputation is an idle and most false imposition, oft got without
merit and lost without deserving. You have lost no reputation at
all, unless you repute yourself such a loser. What, man! There
are ways to recover the general again. You are but now cast   250
in his mood, a punishment more in policy than in malice, even
so as one would beat his offenceless dog to affright an imperious
lion. Sue to him again, and he's yours.

CASSIO I will rather sue to be despised than to deceive so good a
commander with so light, so drunken, and so indiscreet an   255
officer. Drunk! And speak parrot! And squabble! Swagger!
Swear! And discourse fustian with one's own shadow! O thou
invisible spirit of wine, if thou hast no name to be known by, let
us call thee devil!

IAGO What was he that you followed with your sword? What had he   260
done to you?

CASSIO I know not.

IAGO Is't possible?

CASSIO I remember a mass of things, but nothing distinctly: a quarrel,
but nothing wherefore. O God, that men should put an enemy   265
in their mouths to steal away their brains! That we should with joy,
pleasance, revel and applause transform ourselves into beasts!

IAGO Why, but you are now well enough. How came you thus
recovered?

CASSIO It hath pleased the devil drunkenness to give place to the devil   270
wrath; one unperfectness shows me another, to make me frankly
despise myself.

Iago suggests that Cassio should approach Desdemona about his reinstatement. Her good nature and her influence over Othello will restore Cassio to office. Cassio accepts the advice, and promises he will approach Desdemona the next morning.

1 'Had I as many mouths as Hydra' (line 277)

Hydra, a many-headed monster of Greek mythology. New heads grew to replace those which were cut off.

2 What's really in Iago's mind? (in pairs)

Stand back to back and read Iago's speeches from line 281 to line 301. At the end of every phrase or sentence, punctuate Iago's actual words with what he really means. Show what is going on in his mind, his unrevealed thoughts.

---

inordinate superfluous
familiar creature friendly spirit
approved it tested it out

splinter mend (apply a splint)
betimes early

IAGO Come, you are too severe a moraler. As the time, the place, and the condition of this country stands, I could heartily wish this had not befallen; but since it is as it is, mend it for your own good. 275

CASSIO I will ask him for my place again; he shall tell me I am a drunkard. Had I as many mouths as Hydra, such an answer would stop them all. To be now a sensible man, by and by a fool, and presently a beast! O strange! Every inordinate cup is unblessed, and the ingredience is a devil. 280

IAGO Come, come, good wine is a good familiar creature, if it be well used; exclaim no more against it. And, good lieutenant, I think you think I love you.

CASSIO I have well approved it, sir. I drunk!

IAGO You or any man living may be drunk at a time, man. I'll 285 tell you what you shall do. Our general's wife is now the general. I may say so in this respect, for that he hath devoted and given up himself to the contemplation, mark, and denotement of her parts and graces. Confess yourself freely to her, importune her help to put you in your place again. She is of so free, so kind, 290 so apt, so blest a disposition, that she holds it a vice in her goodness not to do more than she is requested. This broken joint between you and her husband entreat her to splinter; and my fortunes against any lay worth naming, this crack of your love shall grow stronger than it was before. 295

CASSIO You advise me well.

IAGO I protest, in the sincerity of love and honest kindness.

CASSIO I think it freely; and betimes in the morning I will beseech the virtuous Desdemona to undertake for me. I am desperate of my fortunes if they check me here. 300

IAGO You are in the right. Good night, lieutenant, I must to the watch.

CASSIO Good night, honest Iago.   *Exit*

Iago spells out his plans to lie to Othello about Desdemona and Cassio having an affair. Her pleading to Othello for Cassio will only make things worse for all three of them. Roderigo tells Iago that he's had enough of 'the chase'.

1 Iago's soliloquy – creating atmosphere (the whole class)

This activity requires a large hall or classroom.

Stand in a large circle and read lines 303–29 through in turn, each person taking a 'chunk' of script – either a sentence or a meaningful phrase. When you have read the speech through once, memorise the piece of script you read out. (Make sure each of you has a different 'chunk' of script.)

One way of learning your piece of Iago's soliloquy is to repeat it over and over again to yourself out loud. Ignore everyone else in the room! Your teacher can suggest ways in which you might say it (for example, shouting, whispering, in the style of a music hall villain, etc.).

Next, reassemble in your circle in the same order as you were before, and speak through the entire speech in the right order. Make sure you remember your cue: the line immediately before yours.

Break up the circle, and scatter all around the room, finding hiding places. Dim the lights if this is possible. One by one, in order, creep out from your hiding place saying your line as you approach the centre of the room. Build up the atmosphere of Iago's developing evil thoughts.

Try variations: decide on the tone of voice you are all going to use to say your respective line (for example, stage whisper, loud and proud!). Or start in whispers, and get louder, building up to the last line. You could try different movements, possibly starting close together, but with each person stealing away from the tight group as they say their line.

Experiment! Find what 'dramatisation' best suits Iago's words and character.

---

probal reasonable
inclining sympathetic
baptism Christian faith
seals and symbols for example, the sign of the cross

divinity study of religion
suggest tempt, seduce
repeals tries to get him reinstated
cudgelled beaten

IAGO And what's he then that says I play the villain,
       When this advice is free I give, and honest,
       Probal to thinking, and indeed the course   305
       To win the Moor again? For 'tis most easy
       Th'inclining Desdemona to subdue
       In any honest suit. She's framed as fruitful
       As the free elements; and then for her
       To win the Moor, were't to renounce his baptism,   310
       All seals and symbols of redeemèd sin,
       His soul is so enfettered to her love,
       That she may make, unmake, do what she list,
       Even as her appetite shall play the god
       With his weak function. How am I then a villain   315
       To counsel Cassio to this parallel course
       Directly to his good? Divinity of hell!
       When devils will the blackest sins put on,
       They do suggest at first with heavenly shows
       As I do now. For whiles this honest fool   320
       Plies Desdemona to repair his fortunes,
       And she for him pleads strongly to the Moor,
       I'll pour this pestilence into his ear:
       That she repeals him for her body's lust;
       And by how much she strives to do him good,   325
       She shall undo her credit with the Moor.
       So will I turn her virtue into pitch,
       And out of her own goodness make the net
       That shall enmesh them all.

                      Enter Roderigo.

                      How now, Roderigo?
RODERIGO I do follow here in the chase, not like a hound that hunts,   330
       but one that fills up the cry. My money is almost spent; I have
       been tonight exceedingly well cudgelled; and I think the issue will
       be, I shall have so much experience for my pains; and so, with
       no money at all, and a little more wit, return again to Venice.

Iago bids Roderigo to be patient and tells him they have already succeeded in disgracing Cassio. Left alone, Iago plans to make Emilia urge Desdemona to help Cassio, then to ensure that Othello sees his wife and Cassio together.

Edmund Kean as Iago (1814). Which lines opposite do you think he might be speaking? Or do you think this pictures him at another point in the play?

dilatory dragging, slow
jump at the very moment
device plot

IAGO How poor are they that have no patience! 335
What wound did ever heal but by degrees?
Thou know'st we work by wit and not by witchcraft,
And wit depends on dilatory time.
Does't not go well? Cassio hath beaten thee,
And thou by that small hurt hath cashiered Cassio. 340
Though other things grow fair against the sun,
Yet fruits that blossom first will first be ripe.
Content thyself awhile. By th'mass, 'tis morning:
Pleasure and action make the hours seem short.
Retire thee, go where thou art billeted. 345
Away, I say, thou shalt know more hereafter –
Nay, get thee gone.

Exit Roderigo

Two things are to be done.
My wife must move for Cassio to her mistress –
I'll set her on.
Myself the while to draw the Moor apart, 350
And bring him jump when he may Cassio find
Soliciting his wife. Ay, that's the way:
Dull not device by coldness and delay.

Exit

Looking back at Act 2

1 Interview Montano (in pairs)

Imagine one of you works for Cyprus Television News. You are conducting an interview of the Governor of Cyprus, questioning him about his views on the future of Cyprus under General Othello, and his opinion of Othello's closest aides.

The other partner is Montano, who has agreed to be interviewed from his hospital bed, following the injuries he sustained during the previous evening's party.

Improvise the interview, and show it to the rest of the class.

2 The storm

The opening scene of Act 2 is dominated by the severe storm threatening the shores of Cyprus. However, in the Italian story by Giraldi Cinthio (from which Shakespeare took the basic idea for his play) the main characters sail to Cyprus on 'a sea of the utmost tranquillity'.

Prepare a talk on Shakespeare's dramatic use of the storm, carefully considering all that has gone on in Act 2.

3 Stage design (in pairs or groups of three)

A director of the play has decided to take the storm as a central image for her production. She has asked you to make a design for a back-drop which will be visible throughout the performance. Using Act 2 Scene 1 as your inspiration (particularly lines 12–17), produce two or three possible designs which could be used.

Can you account for the director's choice of image; why does she regard the storm at sea to be so important?

4 Metaphors

Cassio calls Desdemona 'the riches of the sea' in Scene 1. Here, certain essential qualities which Cassio attributes to Desdemona are pictured graphically for us. This kind of comparison is called a **metaphor**.

Can you create your own appropriate metaphors to describe a particular attribute of Othello, Cassio and Iago? In each case choose an image which is fitting to that person's job, character or outward appearance.

5 Judgements and justice

In both Act 1 and Act 2, a crucial judgement is made and 'justice' publicly dispensed. With a partner, locate each judgement, and the participants in each case. Identify the motive, the 'evidence' presented and the consequences of the ruling made. What key similarities and/or differences are there?

Devise a graphic way of recording your findings on a large sheet of display paper.

6 A production photograph

Below is a photograph taken from John Barton's 1971 Royal Shakespeare Company production of *Othello*, with Brewster Mason as Othello and Lisa Harrow as Desdemona. It shows Iago photographing the wedding party.

Can you suggest where this moment fitted into Act 2, and why you think the director wanted to include a wedding photograph at all?

*Cassio's hired musicians play for Othello and Desdemona. A Clown jokes
with a Musician. Cassio sends the Clown to Emilia, to ask her to come
out and speak with him.*

1 The Clown (in groups of three)

Elizabethan and Jacobean acting companies always employed a comic
actor, or clown. His main role was to play funny parts in plays,
possibly embellishing the given script with 'off-the-cuff' jokes.
Playwrights would generally create a specific role in order to
accommodate the clown, even in tragic plays. One effect (for
example, in *Macbeth*) may be to relieve growing tension in the drama.

Read the page of script aloud. Discuss what you think of the
humour here, for example, the clown's punning on the word 'Naples',
a joke on the nasal sound of a Neapolitan accent, and 'Neapolitan
disease', a venereal disease. Do you think it has any dramatic function
and would you consider it makes good use of a professional comic?
Finally, speculate if there is a popular stage or television comic whom
you would want to cast in the part for a modern production of the
play.

2 Musicians (in pairs)

It was an Elizabethan custom to wake newly-weds with music outside
their bedchamber. Talk together about:

- whether you would open the scene with musicians actually playing
  music on stage
- what alternative stagings might be used
- in a modern production, what music you would choose, and why.

You might be able to think of a particular piece of music or song
which has significant meaning for the characters at this point!

3 Make a director's decision

Lines 1–27 are often cut from productions of the play. Decide
whether you would include them. Try to state at least two reasons
both *for* and *against* their inclusion.

---

content your pains pay you for
  your trouble
quillets puns and word plays

ACT 3   SCENE 1
Cyprus   Outside Desdemona's bedchamber

Enter CASSIO, MUSICIANS *and* CLOWN

CASSIO Masters, play here; I will content your pains.
　　　Something that's brief, and bid 'Good morrow, general.'
　　　　　[They play.]
CLOWN Why, masters, have your instruments been in Naples, that
　　　they speak i'th'nose thus?
I MUSICIAN How, sir, how?　　　　　　　　　　　　　　　　　　5
CLOWN Are these, I pray you, wind instruments?
I MUSICIAN Ay, marry are they, sir.
CLOWN O, thereby hangs a tail.
I MUSICIAN Whereby hangs a tale, sir?
CLOWN Marry, sir, by many a wind instrument that I know. But,　　10
　　　masters, here's money for you; and the general so likes your music
　　　that he desires you, for love's sake, to make no more noise with
　　　it.
I MUSICIAN Well sir, we will not.
CLOWN If you have any music that may not be heard, to't again; but,　　15
　　　as they say, to hear music the general does not greatly care.
I MUSICIAN We have none such, sir.
CLOWN Then put up your pipes in your bag, for I'll away. Go,
　　　vanish into air, away!
　　　　　　　　　　　　　　　　　　　　　Exeunt Musicians
CASSIO Dost thou hear, mine honest friend?　　　　　　　　　　20
CLOWN No, I hear not your honest friend; I hear you.
CASSIO Prithee keep up thy quillets – there's a poor piece of gold for
　　　thee. If the gentlewoman that attends the general's wife be
　　　stirring, tell her there's one Cassio entreats her a little favour of
　　　speech. Wilt thou do this?　　　　　　　　　　　　　　　25
CLOWN She is stirring, sir; if she will stir hither, I shall seem to notify
　　　unto her.
CASSIO Do, good my friend.
　　　　　　　　　　　　　　　　　　　　　　Exit Clown

Iago promises Cassio he will take Othello out of the way for a while, so that Cassio and Emilia can talk freely. Emilia tells Cassio that Othello feels obliged to make an example of him, but intends to reinstate him at a convenient moment.

1 Time (in pairs)

Iago's opening comment, 'You have not been abed then?' suggests that this is the very next morning after the drunken party. Why do you think that Shakespeare makes this point?

- to give the impression that Cassio is too upset to sleep
- to make the action seem to happen very quickly
- to give the play continuity
- to give a sense of urgency to the events
- to keep the party fresh in our minds
- to heighten tension
- to illustrate how astute or cunning Iago is
- it's not a particularly important comment and none of the above apply.

Discuss each of the above options and put them in a 'rank order', with the most important reasons at the top. If you choose the last option, be prepared to defend your choice in detail! Compare your ideas with the rest of the class.

2 Emilia

Read Emilia's lines 39–48. Assess what impression it gives you of her character. You could also consider what it tells you about her relationships with Iago, Cassio, Othello and Desdemona.

---

presently at once
stoutly loyally
great affinity important relations

refuse dismiss
bosom mind, feelings

Enter IAGO.

In happy time, Iago.

IAGO You have not been abed then?

CASSIO Why, no; the day had broke before we parted.   30
    I have made bold, Iago,
    To send in to your wife. My suit to her
    Is that she will to virtuous Desdemona
    Procure me some access.

IAGO   I'll send her to you presently;
    And I'll devise a mean to draw the Moor   35
    Out of the way, that your converse and business
    May be more free.

CASSIO   I humbly thank you for't.

Exit [Iago]

    I never knew a Florentine more kind and honest.

Enter EMILIA.

EMILIA Good morrow, good lieutenant; I am sorry
    For your displeasure; but all will sure be well.   40
    The general and his wife are talking of it,
    And she speaks for you stoutly. The Moor replies
    That he you hurt is of great fame in Cyprus
    And great affinity, and that in wholesome wisdom
    He might not but refuse you; but he protests he loves you,   45
    And needs no other suitor but his likings
    To take the safest occasion by the front
    To bring you in again.

CASSIO   Yet I beseech you,
    If you think fit, or that it may be done,
    Give me advantage of some brief discourse   50
    With Desdemon alone.

EMILIA   Pray you, come in;
    I will bestow you where you shall have time
    To speak your bosom freely.

CASSIO   I am much bound to you.

Exeunt

Othello goes off to inspect the fortifications. In Scene 3 Desdemona assures Cassio that she will help him. Cassio expresses his gratitude.

---

1 Scene 2 (in pairs)

Staging: As you can see at a glance, Scene 2 is extremely short. This might pose particular staging problems (a change of scene for only six lines of dialogue). Discuss what ideas you might have for staging this scene so that it can be included without disrupting the flow of the play. Consider whether you would employ a different way of staging it for a film version of the play as opposed to a theatre production.

How it works: Now, turn your attention to the purpose of Scene 2: its dramatic function(s). For this you need to look back at the previous scene, and glance forward to the beginning of the next. Copy out the diagram below and fill in the relevant information:

	Scene 1	Scene 2	Scene 3
Characters			
What happens?			
How is the plot taken forward?			
Where does it take place?			
Any props needed?			

Study your completed diagram. What can you deduce about the function of Scene 2? Think about the following issues in your discussions:

- Othello's role as a military leader
- Iago's relationship with Othello
- Desdemona's whereabouts
- the time scheme
- Cassio's whereabouts
- Cyprus as a colonial outpost.

---

works ramparts, fortifications
repair return

ACT 3   SCENE 2
Cyprus   Outside the castle

Enter OTHELLO, IAGO *and* GENTLEMEN

OTHELLO These letters give, Iago, to the pilot,
 And by him do my duties to the senate.
 That done, I will be walking on the works;
 Repair there to me.
IAGO   Well, my good lord, I'll do't.   [*Exit*]
OTHELLO This fortification, gentlemen, shall we see't?   5
GENTLEMEN We'll wait upon your lordship.

              Exeunt

ACT 3   SCENE 3
Cyprus   A room in the castle

Enter DESDEMONA, CASSIO *and* EMILIA

DESDEMONA Be thou assured, good Cassio, I will do
 All my abilities in thy behalf.
EMILIA Good madam, do; I warrant it grieves my husband
 As if the case were his.
DESDEMONA O, that's an honest fellow. Do not doubt, Cassio,   5
 But I will have my lord and you again
 As friendly as you were.
CASSIO   Bounteous madam,
 Whatever shall become of Michael Cassio,
 He's never anything but your true servant.
DESDEMONA I know't; I thank you. You do love my lord,   10
 You have known him long, and be you well assured
 He shall in strangeness stand no farther off
 Than in a politic distance.

Cassio fears that Othello may not relent, but Desdemona again pledges her support. Othello sees them in conversation, and Iago draws attention to Cassio's hurried departure.

1 Desdemona's pledge (in pairs)

Desdemona promises to Cassio: 'I give thee warrant of thy place'. She will help him back to his military position on the grounds of personal friendship. Spend about five minutes discussing Desdemona's role here, as friend, wife, woman and civilian. Compare your ideas with the rest of the class.

2 Exits and entrances (in small groups)

The manner and timing of characters' entrances and exits in this moment of the play are crucial to the dramatic development. The Elizabethan or Jacobean stage had a deep acting area with two entrance/exit doors at the back. The size of the acting area would make it possible for Othello and Iago to enter and pass by Cassio at a distance, allowing the remaining dialogue (including Iago's 'Ha! I like not that') to work theatrically.

Turn to the picture of an Elizabethan stage on page 186. It is similar in shape to the Globe Theatre, where *Othello* was performed. Try 'blocking' the moves of all the characters involved between line 25 and line 51. Match the precise entrances and exits with lines of script. Decide how many lines of script it takes, for example, for Cassio to make his exit.

3 'Ha! I like not that'

One student wrote, 'Only Iago could possibly speak line 35. It expresses his character utterly.'

List your reasons for agreeing or disagreeing.

---

warrant promise
watch him keep him awake (a way
  of taming hawks)
board dinner table, meals

shrift confessional, place for
  penance
solicitor advocate, helper

CASSIO   Ay, but, lady,
    That policy may either last so long
    Or feed upon such nice and waterish diet,   15
    Or breed itself so out of circumstance,
    That I being absent and my place supplied,
    My general will forget my love and service.
DESDEMONA Do not doubt that. Before Emilia here,
    I give thee warrant of thy place. Assure thee   20
    If I do vow a friendship, I'll perform it
    To the last article. My lord shall never rest,
    I'll watch him tame and talk him out of patience;
    His bed shall seem a school, his board a shrift;
    I'll intermingle every thing he does   25
    With Cassio's suit. Therefore be merry, Cassio;
    Thy solicitor shall rather die
    Than give thy cause away.

          Enter OTHELLO *and* IAGO.

EMILIA Madam, here comes my lord.
CASSIO Madam, I'll take my leave.   30
DESDEMONA Why, stay and hear me speak.
CASSIO Madam, not now: I am very ill at ease,
    Unfit for mine own purposes.
DESDEMONA Well, do your discretion.

                     Exit Cassio

IAGO Ha! I like not that.
OTHELLO   What dost thou say?   35
IAGO Nothing, my lord; or if – I know not what.
OTHELLO Was not that Cassio parted from my wife?
IAGO Cassio, my lord? No, sure I cannot think it
    That he would steal away so guilty-like,
    Seeing you coming.
OTHELLO   I do believe 'twas he.   40
DESDEMONA How now, my lord?
    I have been talking with a suitor here,
    A man that languishes in your displeasure.
OTHELLO Who is't you mean?

Desdemona playfully lobbies Othello about Cassio's reinstatement. She reminds him that Cassio accompanied Othello during their courtship. Othello agrees Cassio may come to see him at any time.

1 Desdemona's role (in pairs)

Take the parts of Desdemona and Othello and read the script opposite. Several readers of the play have commented that Desdemona shows little understanding of the responsibilities of her husband's position. She confuses personal feelings with official duties and believes that Cassio should be pardoned for a military offence simply because he has been their good friend. Discuss how far you believe Desdemona is justified to plead on Cassio's behalf.

2 Othello's reply

When Othello says, 'I will deny thee nothing' in line 76, what do you think is his manner? Consider the following suggestions in turn. Othello's mood is:

weary	impatient with Desdemona	anxious
condescending	loving and indulgent	angry

Write a paragraph outlining what might be going on in Othello's mind, and how he should utter these words.

3 The eavesdroppers? (in groups of four or five)

When we read the script on the page we tend to forget that characters who have fallen silent are still on stage. Throughout this private exchange between husband and wife there are at least two other characters present. Decide who else is present and then discuss what they might be doing during this dialogue. Indeed, can they hear it?

---

sooth in truth
trespass misdeed

check rebuke
mammering on stuttering

DESDEMONA Why, your lieutenant, Cassio. Good my lord,   45
    If I have any grace or power to move you,
    His present reconciliation take.
    For if he be not one that truly loves you,
    That errs in ignorance, and not in cunning,
    I have no judgement in an honest face.   50
    I prithee call him back.
OTHELLO   Went he hence now?
DESDEMONA Ay, sooth; so humbled
    That he hath left part of his grief with me
    To suffer with him. Good love, call him back.
OTHELLO Not now, sweet Desdemon; some other time.   55
DESDEMONA But shall't be shortly?
OTHELLO   The sooner, sweet, for you.
DESDEMONA Shall't be tonight at supper?
OTHELLO   No, not tonight.
DESDEMONA Tomorrow dinner then?
OTHELLO   I shall not dine at home.
    I meet the captains at the citadel.
DESDEMONA Why, then, tomorrow night, or Tuesday morn,   60
    On Tuesday noon, or night; on Wednesday morn.
    I prithee name the time, but let it not
    Exceed three days. In faith, he's penitent;
    And yet his trespass, in our common reason –
    Save that, they say, the wars must make example   65
    Out of their best – is not almost a fault
    T'incur a private check. When shall he come?
    Tell me, Othello. I wonder in my soul
    What you would ask me that I should deny,
    Or stand so mammering on. What! Michael Cassio,   70
    That came a-wooing with you, and so many a time
    When I have spoke of you dispraisingly
    Hath tane your part, to have so much to do
    To bring him in? By'r Lady, I could do much –
OTHELLO Prithee no more. Let him come when he will;   75
    I will deny thee nothing.

Othello dismisses Desdemona, promising to grant her requests. Iago continues to drop deceptive hints about Cassio. Othello tries to find out what's on Iago's mind.

1 Sowing the seeds of doubt (in groups of three or four)

Right from Cassio's exit and Iago's accompanying 'I like not that' at line 35, Iago manages to plant ideas in Othello's mind without saying very much. Understatement is highly effective and suggestive. Divide up the following lines and work out a dramatic presentation of them. Bring out the insidious way in which Iago works.

Ha! I like not that	Indeed?
No further harm	My Lord, for aught I know
Nothing, my lord;	Honest, my lord?
Or, if . . .	Think, my lord?
No further harm	Cassio, my lord?

2 'Chaos is come again'

For Othello, falling out of love with Desdemona will be literally 'the end of the world'. Some Elizabethans believed that a state of Chaos existed before the creation, and that when the world ended, Chaos would return. It was something to be feared, in the same way that some sections of late twentieth-century society fear world-wide nuclear destruction. Othello's comment might mean that the effects of falling out of love will be personally catastrophic (using cosmic imagery) – or that personal chaos will literally return ('come again') implying that he has experienced such a state of personal disorder once before. Which interpretation do you think is most likely? Are both equally likely?

boon personal favour
peculiar personal

DESDEMONA   Why, this is not a boon;
   'Tis as I should entreat you wear your gloves,
   Or feed on nourishing dishes, or keep you warm,
   Or sue to you to do a peculiar profit
   To your own person. Nay, when I have a suit   80
   Wherein I mean to touch your love indeed,
   It shall be full of poise and difficult weight,
   And fearful to be granted.
OTHELLO   I will deny thee nothing.
   Whereon, I do beseech thee, grant me this,
   To leave me but a little to myself.   85
DESDEMONA Shall I deny you? No; farewell, my lord.
OTHELLO Farewell, my Desdemona, I'll come to thee straight.
DESDEMONA Emilia, come. Be as your fancies teach you;
   Whate'er you be, I am obedient.
                 Exeunt Desdemona and Emilia
OTHELLO Excellent wretch! Perdition catch my soul   90
   But I do love thee; and when I love thee not,
   Chaos is come again.
IAGO   My noble lord –
OTHELLO What dost thou say, Iago?
IAGO   Did Michael Cassio,
   When you wooed my lady, know of your love?
OTHELLO He did from first to last. Why dost thou ask?   95
IAGO But for a satisfaction of my thought;
   No further harm.
OTHELLO   Why of thy thought, Iago?
IAGO I did not think he had been acquainted with her.
OTHELLO O yes, and went between us very oft.
IAGO Indeed?   100
OTHELLO Indeed? Ay, indeed. Discern'st thou aught in that?
   Is he not honest?
IAGO Honest, my lord?
OTHELLO Honest? Ay, honest.   echo.
IAGO My lord, for aught I know.
OTHELLO   What dost thou think?   105
IAGO Think, my lord?
OTHELLO Think, my lord! By heaven, he echoes me,
   As if there were some monster in his thought
   Too hideous to be shown. Thou dost mean something.

Othello presses Iago to reveal his thoughts, assuring him that he knows him to be an honest and faithful man. Iago says he believes Cassio to be honest, but asks to be excused from telling his inner thoughts.

1 Qualified praise (in groups of three)

At line 126, Iago appears to be asserting his confidence in Cassio's honesty. Yet if you look carefully at the exact words he uses, he is cleverly and subtly suggesting the opposite. Start with the basic statement 'he's honest' and see how Iago doubly modifies it with phrases which signal doubt.

Take the following three statements and experiment with ways of presenting them:

- he's honest
- I think he's honest
- I dare be sworn I think he's honest.

2 The false and the just (in small groups)

In lines 118–25, Othello talks of the 'just' man and the 'false' man. He says both can speak in the same style or manner, but from different causes. For a 'false disloyal knave', hesitation in speech is a customary habit. For a 'just' man it arises because he is carefully weighing his words. It is ironic that Othello thinks Iago's 'stops' (hesitations) are a mark of honesty.

But how *do* you know when someone is telling the truth? Talk together about whether you can distinguish between a truthful person and a liar by the way they speak.

---

conceit idea
tricks of custom familiar
  deceptions
close dilations involuntary delays
  (note: there is much disagreement
  about the meaning of this phrase)

ruminate think
leets local courts
law-days days on which courts are
  in session

I heard thee say even now thou lik'st not that, 110
When Cassio left my wife. What didst not like?
And when I told thee he was of my counsel
In my whole course of wooing, thou cried'st 'Indeed?'
And didst contract and purse thy brow together,
As if thou then hadst shut up in thy brain 115
Some horrible conceit. If thou dost love me,
Show me thy thought.

IAGO My lord, you know I love you.

OTHELLO   I think thou dost;
And for I know thou'rt full of love and honesty,
And weigh'st thy words before thou giv'st them breath, 120
Therefore these stops of thine fright me the more;
For such things in a false disloyal knave
Are tricks of custom; but in a man that's just,
They're close dilations, working from the heart,
That passion cannot rule.

IAGO   For Michael Cassio, 125
I dare be sworn I think that he is honest.

OTHELLO I think so too.

IAGO   Men should be what they seem;
Or those that be not, would they might seem none!

OTHELLO Certain, men should be what they seem.

IAGO Why then, I think Cassio's an honest man. 130

OTHELLO Nay, yet there's more in this.
I prithee speak to me as to thy thinkings,
As thou dost ruminate, and give thy worst of thoughts
The worst of words.

IAGO   Good my lord, pardon me;
Though I am bound to every act of duty, 135
I am not bound to that all slaves are free to.
Utter my thoughts! Why, say they are vile and false?
As where's that palace, whereinto foul things
Sometimes intrude not? Who has a breast so pure,
But some uncleanly apprehensions 140
Keep leets and law-days, and in session sit
With meditations lawful?

Othello

*Iago continues to seem reluctant to reveal what he claims to know about
Cassio and Desdemona. He strongly defends the importance of a man's
or woman's reputation, and warns Othello to beware of jealousy.*

1 Sculptures of Trust and Jealousy (in groups of three)

One person takes on the job of sculptor, whilst the remaining two
people become the raw material. The sculptor's task is to create,
firstly, a statue entitled 'Trust' and secondly, one entitled 'Jealousy'.

2 'Good name . . . the jewel of their souls'
(in groups of four or five)

Read through Iago's statement about 'good name' or reputation (lines
156–62). Work out a short improvisation which seems to you to
explain the central meaning of these lines.

3 'The green-eyed monster'

Spend some time analysing Iago's definition of jealousy (lines 168–9).
How appropriate is the image as a whole? (Consider colour, shape
and action.) Describe in detail what picture it conjures up in your
mind. Try to sketch it.

4 Game tactics (in groups of three)

Iago approaches his task tactically. It is as intriguing following his
verbal 'moves' as it can be monitoring a good game of tennis or
snooker, where each individual move is part of a much wider game
strategy.

One of you now becomes a commentator on the game and the
other two take the parts of Iago and Othello. Read aloud lines
143–78. Present the dialogue as it were a game being watched by a
radio commentator. The commentator can interrupt wherever it
seems most appropriate to do so!

---

my nature's plague I can't help it
conceits imagines
**scattering and unsure
  observance** random and
  uncertain perceptions

quiet peace of mind
cuckold wronged husband
dotes loves

OTHELLO Thou dost conspire against thy friend, Iago,
        If thou but think'st him wronged, and mak'st his ear
        A stranger to thy thoughts.
IAGO   I do beseech you,   145
        Though I perchance am vicious in my guess –
        As I confess it is my nature's plague
        To spy into abuses, and oft my jealousy
        Shapes faults that are not – that your wisdom then,
        From one that so imperfectly conceits,   150
        Would take no notice, nor build yourself a trouble
        Out of his scattering and unsure observance.
        It were not for your quiet, nor your good,
        Nor for my manhood, honesty, and wisdom,
        To let you know my thoughts.
OTHELLO   What dost thou mean?   155
IAGO Good name in man and woman, dear my lord,
        Is the immediate jewel of their souls.
        Who steals my purse, steals trash; 'tis something,
            nothing,
        'Twas mine, 'tis his, and has been slave to thousands:
        But he that filches from me my good name   160
        Robs me of that which not enriches him
        And makes me poor indeed.
OTHELLO By heaven, I'll know thy thoughts.
IAGO You cannot, if my heart were in your hand,
        Nor shall not, while 'tis in my custody.   165
OTHELLO Ha!
IAGO O beware, my lord, of jealousy:
        It is the green-eyed monster which doth mock
        The meat it feeds on. That cuckold lives in bliss
        Who certain of his fate loves not his wronger;   170
        But O, what damnèd minutes tells he o'er
        Who dotes, yet doubts, suspects, yet fondly loves?
OTHELLO O misery!

Othello

Othello assures Iago he's not a naturally jealous man. He says he is confident of his wife's virtue. Iago warns him to watch Desdemona with Cassio; she is capable of deception.

1 Key words (in groups of three)

Read lines 178–206. Between you, agree on what seems to be the key word on each line. Now, working only with those words you have chosen, experiment with ways of presenting the exchange between Iago and Othello. You could 'intercut' (interweave) the two sets of key words, for example, if you feel that contributes to an understanding of the dynamics of the dialogue. Involve all three members of the group, making use of any dramatic approach which seems to be most appropriate to you. Compare your presentation with those of other groups. Discuss major areas of similarity or difference.

Ian McKellen as Iago and Willard White as Othello in Trevor Nunn's Royal Shakespeare Company production (1989).

---

fineless endless
goat goats were supposed to be particularly lecherous

exsufflicate exaggerated
self-bounty natural generosity and kindness

IAGO Poor and content is rich, and rich enough;
          But riches fineless is as poor as winter   175
          To him that ever fears he shall be poor.
          Good God, the souls of all my tribe defend
          From jealousy.
OTHELLO   Why, why is this?
          Think'st thou I'd make a life of jealousy,
          To follow still the changes of the moon   180
          With fresh suspicions? No, to be once in doubt
          Is once to be resolved. Exchange me for a goat
          When I shall turn the business of my soul
          To such exsufflicate and blown surmises
          Matching thy inference. 'Tis not to make me jealous   185
          To say my wife is fair, feeds well, loves company,
          Is free of speech, sings, plays, and dances well:
          Where virtue is, these are more virtuous.
          Nor from mine own weak merits will I draw
          The smallest fear or doubt of her revolt,   190
          For she had eyes and chose me. No, Iago,
          I'll see before I doubt; when I doubt, prove;
          And on the proof, there is no more but this:
          Away at once with love or jealousy!
IAGO I am glad of this; for now I shall have reason   195
          To show the love and duty that I bear you
          With franker spirit. Therefore, as I am bound,
          Receive it from me. I speak not yet of proof.
          Look to your wife, observe her well with Cassio;
          Wear your eyes thus: not jealous, nor secure.   200
          I would not have your free and noble nature,
          Out of self-bounty, be abused. Look to't.
          I know our country disposition well:
          In Venice they do let God see the pranks
          They dare not show their husbands. Their best
             conscience   205
          Is not to leave't undone, but keep't unknown.

Iago reminds Othello that Desdemona has already deceived her father.
He professes his love for Othello, but continues to drop hints about
Desdemona's lack of fidelity, and to heighten Othello's unease.

1 Who's deceiving who?

Iago has already commented (lines 203–06) on Venetian women's ability to deceive. Now, his 'She did deceive her father, marrying you . . .' closely echoes Brabantio's parting words in Act 1, Scene 3, lines 288–9. See if you can devise a diagrammatic way of representing which characters are being deceived by Iago at this point, and who believes he or she is being deceived by others! For each 'strand' of your diagram, try to find a relevant quotation and include that in your design.

2 Iago the racist? (in pairs)

One student wrote that she saw Iago as a typical white racist: 'on the surface happy to work with a black colleague, but underneath unable to contemplate fully equal relations'. Is there anything in Iago's words on the page opposite which leads you to agree with her point? Do you think that such a view helps to explain Iago's motivation to plot against Othello, either wholly or partly?

3 'I am bound to thee for ever'

Does Othello speak more truly than he knows in line 215? Advise the two actors how they might bring out the meanings of this line to make the greatest impact on the audience.

---

seel stitch up
close as oak like the close grain of
  an oak tree

strain push further
larger reach go beyond
success result

OTHELLO Dost thou say so?
IAGO She did deceive her father, marrying you;
     And when she seemed to shake and fear your looks
     She loved them most.
OTHELLO   And so she did.
IAGO   Why, go to then!   210
     She that so young could give out such a seeming
     To seel her father's eyes up close as oak
     He thought 'twas witchcraft – but I am much to blame,
     I humbly do beseech you of your pardon
     For too much loving you.
OTHELLO   I am bound to thee for ever.   215
IAGO I see this hath a little dashed your spirits.
OTHELLO Not a jot, not a jot.
IAGO   I'faith, I fear it has.
     I hope you will consider what is spoke
     Comes from my love. But I do see you're moved.
     I am to pray you not to strain my speech   220
     To grosser issues nor to larger reach
     Than to suspicion.
OTHELLO I will not.
IAGO   Should you do so, my lord,
     My speech should fall into such vile success
     As my thoughts aimed not at. Cassio's my worthy
         friend –   225
     My lord, I see you're moved.
OTHELLO   No, not much moved.
     I do not think but Desdemona's honest.
IAGO Long live she so, and long live you to think so!
OTHELLO And yet how nature erring from itself –

Othello

Iago implies the unnaturalness of Desdemona in preferring a black man over someone of her own colour and society. Othello orders Iago to set Emilia to watch Desdemona. Iago advises Othello to see how Desdemona pleads for Cassio's reinstatement.

1 'Honest creature' (in groups of four to six)

Create a tableau or short mime called 'The honest creature' – aim at an ironic interpretation of the title! Share your ideas with the rest of the class.

2 Natural? (in small groups)

Iago's 'in all things nature tends' (line 233) echoes Othello's 'And yet how nature erring from itself' (line 229). But is Desdemona's marriage to Othello unnatural? Talk together about whether history has changed people's views on inter-racial marrriage.

James Earl Jones as Othello and Christopher Plummer as Iago (Broadway, 1981–2).

affect like	**means** methods
clime country	**strain his entertainment** urges
disproportion impropriety	his reinstatement
fall to match come to compare	**importunity** pleading
country forms own countrymen	**government** self-control
happily perhaps	

IAGO Ay, there's the point: as, to be bold with you,   230
    Not to affect many proposèd matches
    Of her own clime, complexion, and degree,
    Whereto we see in all things nature tends –
    Foh! one may smell, in such, a will most rank,
    Foul disproportion, thoughts unnatural.   235
    But pardon me: I do not in position
    Distinctly speak of her; though I may fear
    Her will, recoiling to her better judgement,
    May fall to match you with her country forms,
    And happily repent.
OTHELLO   Farewell, farewell.   240
    If more thou dost perceive, let me know more;
    Set on thy wife to observe. Leave me, Iago.
IAGO [*Going.*] My lord, I take my leave.
OTHELLO Why did I marry? This honest creature doubtless
    Sees and knows more, much more, than he unfolds.   245
IAGO [*Returning.*] My lord, I would I might entreat your honour
    To scan this thing no farther. Leave it to time.
    Although 'tis fit that Cassio have his place –
    For sure he fills it up with great ability –
    Yet if you please to hold him off awhile,   250
    You shall by that perceive him and his means.
    Note if your lady strain his entertainment
    With any strong or vehement importunity –
    Much will be seen in that. In the mean time,
    Let me be thought too busy in my fears –   255
    As worthy cause I have to fear I am –
    And hold her free, I do beseech your honour.
OTHELLO Fear not my government.
IAGO I once more take my leave.   *Exit*

Othello reflects that his colour, speech and age may have lost him Desdemona. He sees women's unfaithfulness as the curse of marriage. But the sight of Desdemona seems to make him reject his suspicions.

1 Marriage guidance (in pairs)

Work in detail on Othello's soliloquy (lines 260–79). Imagine Othello is consulting a marriage guidance counsellor at this point. One partner reads Othello's speech, the other punctuates it where appropriate with suitable, down-to-earth words of advice. For example:

OTHELLO   This fellow's of exceeding honesty . . .
COUNSELLOR   Are you really sure? I mean, how do you know he's one hundred per cent trustworthy?
OTHELLO   [he] knows all qualities, with a learnèd spirit Of human dealings . . .

2 Hawking imagery

Using trained hawks for hunting small prey was a courtly pursuit in Elizabethan times. Othello uses a number of hawking images in his soliloquy about Desdemona. He wonders if she will prove to be a 'haggard' (a wild, untrained hawk) in which case he will set her free ('whistle her off') and untie the 'jesses' (the straps tied round the hawk's legs). He will 'let her down the wind/To prey at fortune', in other words, let her go to look after herself.

Write a paragraph explaining how appropriate you find this image to be. Show if you think it is effective, given the character and mood of Othello and Desdemona. Does it reveal anything about the way Othello regards marriage?

---

haply for perhaps because
chamberers gallants, young men
vapour stinking air
prerogatived privileged

forkèd plague cuckold's horns (the mark of deceived husbands)
do quicken are born

OTHELLO This fellow's of exceeding honesty   260
And knows all qualities, with a learnèd spirit,
Of human dealings. If I do prove her haggard,
Though that her jesses were my dear heart-strings,
I'd whistle her off and let her down the wind
To prey at fortune. Haply for I am black,   265
And have not those soft parts of conversation
That chamberers have, or for I am declined
Into the vale of years – yet that's not much –
She's gone, I am abused, and my relief
Must be to loathe her. O curse of marriage,   270
That we can call these delicate creatures ours
And not their appetites! I had rather be a toad
And live upon the vapour of a dungeon
Than keep a corner in the thing I love
For others' uses. Yet 'tis the plague of great ones,   275
Prerogatived are they less than the base;
'Tis destiny unshunnable, like death:
Even then this forkèd plague is fated to us
When we do quicken. Look where she comes.

Enter Desdemona and Emilia.

If she be false, O then heaven mocks itself;   280
I'll not believe it.

Desdemona greets Othello, who claims he has a headache. She tries to bind his head with her handkerchief, but he pushes it aside. Emilia picks it up, remembering that Iago has urged her to steal it.

1 'I am to blame' (in groups of four)

Discuss what reasons Othello might have to claim that he is to blame – and to blame for what? Elect one person from your group to role-play Othello explaining his reasons for blaming himself at that precise moment. Spend a couple of minutes running through the explanation, then swap 'Othellos'! Send each 'Othello' to another group so that 'he' can explain his reasons to them.

As a whole class, discuss any differences in interpretation that have arisen.

2 Why does Iago want the napkin?

As Emilia holds the handkerchief she reflects that Iago 'hath a hundred times wooed me to steal it'. Why?

Predict what Iago might want to do with Desdemona's handkerchief. What indications are there that this seemingly insignificant object will prove to be of great importance later on?

watching lack of sleep, being on duty
remembrance keepsake

conjured her made her swear
work tane out the embroidery copied

DESDEMONA How now, my dear Othello?
  Your dinner and the generous islanders,
  By you invited, do attend your presence.
OTHELLO I am to blame.
DESDEMONA Why do you speak so faintly?
  Are you not well? 285
OTHELLO I have a pain upon my forehead here.
DESDEMONA Faith, that's with watching; 'twill away again.
  Let me but bind it hard, within this hour
  It will be well.
OTHELLO Your napkin is too little.
  [*He puts the handkerchief from him, and she drops it.*]
  Let it alone. Come, I'll go in with you. 290
DESDEMONA I am very sorry that you are not well.
                      Exeunt Othello and Desdemona
EMILIA I am glad I have found this napkin:
  This was her first remembrance from the Moor.
  My wayward husband hath a hundred times
  Wooed me to steal it; but she so loves the token, 295
  For he conjured her she should ever keep it,
  That she reserves it evermore about her
  To kiss and talk to. I'll have the work tane out
  And give't Iago.
  What he will do with it, heaven knows, not I: 300
  I nothing but to please his fantasy.

Emilia hands the handkerchief over to her husband. Iago reveals to the audience what he intends to do with it.

---

1 Direct Iago and Emilia (in groups of three)

Lines 302–21 present an interesting exchange between husband and wife. It is quite possible to direct it so as to bring out varying interpretations of the relationship between Iago and Emilia. You could even make an important statement about the institution of marriage as it's presented in the play.

Organise yourselves so that one person directs the other two, who take the two acting parts. You will have to make decisions about Emilia's mood and the way she approaches her husband. For example, would you say that Emilia is:

- nervous of Iago
- cheerful
- confident
- resentful and moody
- frustrated
- playfully coquettish
- desperate for her husband to pay her attention.

You may find it useful in your discussions to know that the word 'thing' in Elizabethan slang was used for the female sexual organ. Does Emilia knowingly use it in this sense (line 303) or is Iago introducing the obscene meaning (line 304)? Consider how Emilia would relinquish the napkin according to your interpretation of the mood of the exchange. Decide at precisely what point she would reveal the handkerchief to Iago. How does she leave the stage at line 321?

Experiment with variations. Throughout your explorations you will be closely considering a whole range of issues to do with characterisation, relationships, themes and theatricality.

---

be not acknown on't say you know
  nothing about it
holy writ the Bible
conceits imaginings

Enter Iago.

IAGO How now? What do you here alone?
EMILIA Do not you chide; I have a thing for you.
IAGO You have a thing for me? It is a common thing –
EMILIA Ha!   305
IAGO To have a foolish wife.
EMILIA O, is that all? What will you give me now
    For that same handkerchief?
IAGO   What handkerchief?
EMILIA What handkerchief!
    Why, that the Moor first gave to Desdemona,   310
    That which so often you did bid me steal.
IAGO Hast stolen it from her?
EMILIA No, faith; she let it drop by negligence,
    And to th'advantage I being here took't up.
    Look, here it is.
IAGO   A good wench! Give it me.   315
EMILIA What will you do with't, that you have been so earnest
    To have me filch it?
IAGO [*Snatching it.*]   Why, what's that to you?
EMILIA If it be not for some purpose of import,
    Give't me again. Poor lady, she'll run mad
    When she shall lack it.
IAGO   Be not acknown on't: 320
    I have use for it. Go, leave me.

                          Exit Emilia

    I will in Cassio's lodging lose this napkin
    And let him find it. Trifles light as air
    Are to the jealous confirmations strong
    As proofs of holy writ. This may do something.   325
    The Moor already changes with my poison:
    Dangerous conceits are in their natures poisons,
    Which at the first are scarce found to distaste
    But, with a little act upon the blood,
    Burn like the mines of sulphur. I did say so.   330

Othello is convinced of Desdemona's infidelity. He wishes he were ignorant of it and declares he has lost interest in his life as a professional soldier. He demands that Iago provide him with hard evidence.

1 Ignorance is bliss

Study the page of script and pick out all the lines of Othello's which could be paraphrased as 'ignorance is bliss'.

2 Othello's 'general camp' speech
(in groups of ten or twelve)

a One member of the group reads lines 346–58 aloud. The rest of the group listen carefully and echo any words to do with the military activity.

b Split up the speech (from line 349) between group members. Each person takes one or two lines or meaningful phrases. Learn your respective 'chunks' of text.

c Using mime or tableau(x) or choral speech, present a group version of the speech entitled, 'Othello's occupation's gone'.

3 'Is't come to this?' (in pairs)

In your own words say what you think the situation has 'come to' (line 364) from your own perspective. Next, each partner should take the role of either Iago or Othello and briefly explain what they believe or hope the situation has 'come to'.

4 'Ocular proof'

Decide what kind of things Othello could mean by 'ocular proof' in line 361 (ocular = to do with eyes). Can you detect any inconsistencies in the way Othello is thinking? Turn to a partner and spend three or four minutes comparing your ideas.

---

poppy, mandragora sleep-inducing drugs from plants
thou owed'st was yours
general camp the whole army
pioners men of lowest rank

trump trumpet
circumstance ceremony
engines cannons
clamours thunder

Enter Othello.

Look where he comes! Not poppy nor mandragora,
Nor all the drowsy syrups of the world,
Shall ever medicine thee to that sweet sleep
Which thou owed'st yesterday.

OTHELLO   Ha, ha, false to me!

IAGO Why, how now, general! No more of that.   335

OTHELLO Avaunt, be gone! Thou hast set me on the rack.
I swear 'tis better to be much abused
Than but to know't a little.

IAGO   How now, my lord!

OTHELLO What sense had I of her stolen hours of lust?
I saw't not, thought it not, it harmed not me.   340
I slept the next night well, fed well, was free and merry;
I found not Cassio's kisses on her lips.
He that is robbed, not wanting what is stolen,
Let him not know't and he's not robbed at all.

IAGO I am sorry to hear this.   345

OTHELLO I had been happy if the general camp,
Pioners and all, had tasted her sweet body
So I had nothing known. O, now for ever
Farewell the tranquil mind! Farewell content!
Farewell the plumèd troops, and the big wars   350
That makes ambition virtue – O farewell!
Farewell the neighing steed and the shrill trump,
The spirit-stirring drum, th'ear-piercing fife,
The royal banner, and all quality,
Pride, pomp, and circumstance of glorious war!   355
And, O you mortal engines, whose rude throats
Th'immortal Jove's dread clamours counterfeit,
Farewell! Othello's occupation's gone.

IAGO Is't possible, my lord?

OTHELLO Villain, be sure thou prove my love a whore;   360
Be sure of it. Give me the ocular proof,
Or by the worth of mine eternal soul,
Thou hadst been better have been born a dog
Than answer my waked wrath!

IAGO   Is't come to this?

> *Othello curses Iago if his suspicions are without foundation. Iago protests*
> *that he was only acting as a friend and asks what proof Othello requires*
> *of his wife's infidelity.*

1 Wounded innocence! (in groups of three to five)

Take Iago's speech, 'O grace! O heaven . . .' (lines 374–81). Read it
through in a variety of ways, experimenting with which sounds best to
you. Then choose one key line or phrase each (so that each group
member has a different one) and present an improvisation in which
each person may only use their chosen phrase/line (which can be split
up and repeated as required).

2 Othello's dilemma (in pairs)

Read Othello's lines 384–91. Present the speech as if it were an
argument between two people, splitting up the lines as seems most
appropriate.

3 'Honesty's a fool'

Consider how far Iago's phrase could be regarded as central to the
play as a whole so far. Prepare a short talk, outlining your views and
deliver it either to the rest of the class, or to a group of five or six other
students.

4 Jealousy (in groups of four)

Use your own experience to talk together about how far you agree
with Iago (lines 323–5):

'. . . Trifles light as air
Are to the jealous confirmations strong
As proofs of holy writ.'

---

probation proof
office job, appointment
profit lesson
sith since

Dian goddess of virginity
satisfied certain
topped with a man on top of her

OTHELLO Make me to see't; or, at the least, so prove it   365
    That the probation bear no hinge nor loop
    To hang a doubt on – or woe upon thy life!
IAGO My noble lord –
OTHELLO If thou dost slander her and torture me,
    Never pray more; abandon all remorse;   370
    On horror's head horrors accumulate;
    Do deeds to make heaven weep, all earth amazed:
    For nothing canst thou to damnation add
    Greater than that.
IAGO   O grace! O heaven forgive me!
    Are you a man? Have you a soul? Or sense?   375
    God bu'y you; take mine office. O wretched fool,
    That lov'st to make thine honesty a vice!
    O monstrous world! Take note, take note, O world!
    To be direct and honest is not safe.
    I thank you for this profit, and from hence   380
    I'll love no friend, sith love breeds such offence.
OTHELLO Nay, stay: thou shouldst be honest.
IAGO I should be wise; for honesty's a fool
    And loses that it works for.
OTHELLO   By the world,
    I think my wife be honest, and think she is not;   385
    I think that thou art just, and think thou art not.
    I'll have some proof. Her name, that was as fresh
    As Dian's visage, is now begrimed and black
    As mine own face. If there be cords or knives,
    Poison or fire or suffocating streams,   390
    I'll not endure it. Would I were satisfied!
IAGO I see, sir, you are eaten up with passion.
    I do repent me that I put it to you.
    You would be satisfied?
OTHELLO   Would? Nay, I will.
IAGO And may. But how? How satisfied, my lord?   395
    Would you, the supervisor, grossly gape on?
    Behold her topped?
OTHELLO   Death and damnation! O!

Iago warns that it will be impossible to catch Desdemona and Cassio in the act of adultery. He reports that he has heard Cassio talk of Desdemona in his sleep. Othello threatens murder.

1 Imaginary scene (in pairs)

Iago describes Cassio's nocturnal ramblings in the barrack-room (lines 411–27). Taking the parts of Cassio and Iago act out the imaginary scene as Iago describes it!

2 Agony aunt

Othello's threat to 'tear her all to pieces' is one way of dealing with a case of suspected adultery, but not one to be recommended! Firstly, as a class, discuss what alternative courses of action you would advise someone in Othello's position to take. Next, write a letter to an agony aunt, as if from Othello. In doing so, try to use the kind of style and tone that Othello might well use (be particularly aware, for example, of the kind of vocabulary and imagery he has been using over the last few pages). In your letter don't forget to briefly set the scene and then lay out your immediate concerns. What kind of advice might Othello be after? How would Othello sign off in order to retain his anonymity in case his letter is published? ('Vexed of Venice', for example?)

Exchange your finished letter with a partner and write the agony aunt's reply.

3 Animal instincts

What effect does Iago's talk of animals on heat (lines 404–5) have on you as a reader? Make some suggestions as to the possible significance it might have in the context of the play.

---

bolster share a pillow
prime lecherous
salt lustful

in pride on heat
gripe grasp

IAGO It were a tedious difficulty, I think,
　　　To bring them to that prospect. Damn them then,
　　　If ever mortal eyes do see them bolster　　　　　　400
　　　More than their own. What then? How then?
　　　What shall I say? Where's satisfaction?
　　　It is impossible you should see this,
　　　Were they as prime as goats, as hot as monkeys,
　　　As salt as wolves in pride, and fools as gross　　405
　　　As Ignorance made drunk. But yet, I say,
　　　If imputation and strong circumstances,
　　　Which lead directly to the door of truth,
　　　Will give you satisfaction, you might have't.
OTHELLO Give me a living reason she's disloyal.　　　410
IAGO I do not like the office;
　　　But sith I am entered in this cause so far –
　　　Pricked to't by foolish honesty and love –
　　　I will go on. I lay with Cassio lately,
　　　And being troubled with a raging tooth　　　　　415
　　　I could not sleep.
　　　There are a kind of men so loose of soul
　　　That in their sleeps will mutter their affairs.
　　　One of this kind is Cassio.
　　　In sleep I heard him say, 'Sweet Desdemona,　　420
　　　Let us be wary, let us hide our loves.'
　　　And then, sir, he would gripe and wring my hand,
　　　Cry, 'O sweet creature!' and then kiss me hard,
　　　As if he plucked up kisses by the roots
　　　That grew upon my lips; then laid his leg　　　　425
　　　Over my thigh, and sighed, and kissed, and then
　　　Cried, 'Cursèd fate that gave thee to the Moor.'
OTHELLO O monstrous, monstrous!
IAGO　　　　　　　　　　　　Nay, this was but his dream.
OTHELLO But this denoted a foregone conclusion.
IAGO 'Tis a shrewd doubt, though it be but a dream;　430
　　　And this may help to thicken other proofs
　　　That do demonstrate thinly.
OTHELLO　　　　　　　　　　I'll tear her all to pieces!

Iago claims that Cassio has Desdemona's handkerchief. Othello is overcome with jealous grief and vows revenge. To Iago's call for patience, Othello replies his murderous thoughts will never change.

1 Proof (in pairs)

Othello greets Iago's comment about the handkerchief with the words, 'Now do I see 'tis true'. Yet Othello had asked for 'ocular proof'. Talk together about how Iago has managed to manipulate Othello to accept his *word*.

2 Tableaux (in groups of three)

Express the following images through tableaux.

a 'Arise, black vengeance, from thy hollow cell!'
  Use a series of two or three linked tableaux here.
b 'Yield up, O love, thy crown and hearted throne
  To tyrannous hate!'

3 The tidal wave of Othello's emotions (in large groups)

You need to work in groups of around ten for this activity. It can be a pretty lively and noisy exercise, so be warned! Divide up Othello's 'Pontic Sea' speech (lines 454–63) into small, meaningful 'chunks' (lines or phrases) and distribute amongst your group members. Memorise your lines. Get into a long line, not necessarily facing the same way, and link arms securely. The two students on either end must tug and pull the line around the room in opposite directions. Try this out, shouting the lines you've learnt. You could also add some stirring music. Turn the sound up as loud as you can bear and hurl your words out over it.

Afterwards, discuss what insights this activity has given you into Othello's state of mind at this point in the play, and how the style of his language reflects his thoughts and feelings.

---

hearted in my heart
fraught burden, cargo
aspic venomous snake
Pontic Sea Black Sea

Propontic Sea of Marmora
Hellespont Dardenelles
capable ample

IAGO Nay, yet be wise; yet we see nothing done,
   She may be honest yet. Tell me but this:
   Have you not sometimes seen a handkerchief   435
   Spotted with strawberries in your wife's hand?
OTHELLO I gave her such a one; 'twas my first gift.
IAGO I know not that; but such a handkerchief –
   I am sure it was your wife's – did I today
   See Cassio wipe his beard with.
OTHELLO   If it be that –   440
IAGO If it be that, or any that was hers,
   It speaks against her with the other proofs.
OTHELLO O that the slave had forty thousand lives!
   One is too poor, too weak, for my revenge.
   Now do I see 'tis true. Look here, Iago,   445
   All my fond love thus do I blow to heaven;
   'Tis gone.
   Arise, black vengeance, from thy hollow cell!
   Yield up, O love, thy crown and hearted throne
   To tyrannous hate! Swell, bosom, with thy fraught, 450
   For 'tis of aspics' tongues.
          He kneels.
IAGO   Yet be content.
OTHELLO O, blood, blood, blood!
IAGO Patience, I say; your mind perhaps may change.
OTHELLO Never, Iago. Like to the Pontic Sea,
   Whose icy current and compulsive course   455
   Ne'er feels retiring ebb but keeps due on
   To the Propontic and the Hellespont,
   Even so my bloody thoughts with violent pace
   Shall ne'er look back, ne'er ebb to humble love,
   Till that a capable and wide revenge   460
   Swallow them up. Now by yond marble heaven,
   In the due reverence of a sacred vow
   I here engage my words.

Iago swears to serve Othello, who instructs him to kill Cassio. Othello vows to kill Desdemona himself. He appoints Iago to be his lieutenant. Scene 4 opens with Desdemona sending a messenger to Cassio.

1 'Let her live' (in pairs)

Why do you think Iago tells Othello to let Desdemona live (line 475)? Consider the following possibilities:

- he has no quarrel with Desdemona
- he is only after Cassio's death
- he fancies Desdemona
- he's displaying old-fashioned courtesy towards women
- he needs her alive to torment Othello further
- he actually means the opposite – he's planting the idea deliberately in Othello's mind
- he wants to torment Desdemona more
- it's all happening too quickly and easily
- he wants to appear merciful to aid his deception.

Compare your ideas with the rest of the class.

2 What does Iago mean?

Scene 3 ends on Iago's statement, 'I am your own for ever'. On its most innocent level, this could simply mean 'thanks for the promotion, I'll serve you well'. But what other, more ominous meanings could his words carry, coming as they do at the end of the scene in which Iago has successfully stirred Othello to hatred and jealousy?

3 Opening the scene

If you were directing the play, what dramatic effect would you hope to achieve at the opening of Scene 4. Would you want a swift or slow change of scene? What would Desdemona's mood be, and how would she and the Clown speak? Write a paragraph of director's notes spanning Scene 3, line 480 to Scene 4, line 18.

---

clip enclose, embrace
execution activities

IAGO   Do not rise yet.

He kneels.

     Witness you ever-burning lights above,
     You elements that clip us round about,   465
     Witness that here Iago doth give up
     The execution of his wit, hands, heart,
     To wronged Othello's service. Let him command,
     And to obey shall be in me remorse,
     What bloody business ever.

[They rise.]

OTHELLO   I greet thy love,   470
     Not with vain thanks, but with acceptance bounteous;
     And will upon the instant put thee to't.
     Within these three days let me hear thee say
     That Cassio's not alive.

IAGO   My friend is dead;
     'Tis done at your request. But let her live.   475

OTHELLO Damn her, lewd minx! O, damn her, damn her!
     Come, go with me apart. I will withdraw
     To furnish me with some swift means of death
     For the fair devil. Now art thou my lieutenant.

IAGO I am your own for ever.   480

                                       Exeunt

ACT 3   SCENE 4
Cyprus   A room in the castle

Enter DESDEMONA, EMILIA and CLOWN

DESDEMONA Do you know, sirrah, where Lieutenant Cassio lies?

CLOWN I dare not say he lies anywhere.

DESDEMONA Why, man?

CLOWN He's a soldier, and for one to say a soldier lies is
     stabbing.   5

The Clown leaves to tell Cassio to visit Desdemona. She expresses concern about the loss of her handkerchief to Emilia. Othello greets Desdemona and comments on her hot hand.

1 Interview Emilia (in pairs)

When Emilia claims she knows nothing about the loss of Desdemona's handkerchief ('I know not, madam', line 20) what might be going through her mind at that point?

Explore Emilia's possible motives. Try to work out where her loyalties lie. Then conduct an interview, taking on the roles of the Interviewer and Emilia. Discuss Emilia's position as wife, employee and confidante.

2 Sweaty palms (in groups of two to four)

Othello takes Desdemona's hand and remarks that it is 'hot, and moist' – supposedly a sign of a lecherous nature. He goes on to tell Desdemona that instead of giving her 'hand' in marriage as a love match ('hearts of old gave hands') she has merely given her hand, not her heart as well (lines 41–3).

Read lines 28–43, then improvise a situation where you wrongly (and privately) suspect your girl/boyfriend of two-timing you, and all sorts of quite innocent conversation and behaviour become misinterpreted. After watching each other's improvisations discuss how easily this kind of situation arises, and under what circumstances.

---

devise make up, invent
edified instructed
catechise a method of religious
 instruction
compass scope
crusadoes gold coins

humours moods
dissemble hide one's true feelings
sequester removal
castigation discipline

DESDEMONA Go to. Where lodges he?

CLOWN To tell you where he lodges is to tell you where I lie.

DESDEMONA Can anything be made of this?

CLOWN I know not where he lodges, and for me to devise a lodging, 10
and say he lies here, or he lies there, were to lie in mine own
throat.

DESDEMONA Can you enquire him out, and be edified by report?

CLOWN I will catechise the world for him: that is, make questions,
and by them answer.

DESDEMONA Seek him; bid him come hither; tell him I have moved 15
my lord on his behalf and hope all will be well.

CLOWN To do this is within the compass of man's wit, and therefore
I will attempt the doing of it.   *Exit*

DESDEMONA Where should I lose that handkerchief, Emilia?

EMILIA I know not, madam.   20

DESDEMONA Believe me, I had rather lose my purse
Full of crusadoes; and but my noble Moor
Is true of mind and made of no such baseness
As jealous creatures are, it were enough
To put him to ill thinking.

EMILIA   Is he not jealous?   25

DESDEMONA Who, he? I think the sun where he was born
Drew all such humours from him.

Enter OTHELLO.

EMILIA   Look where he comes.

DESDEMONA I will not leave him now; let Cassio
Be called to him. – How is't with you, my lord?

OTHELLO Well, my good lady. [*Aside*] O hardness to dissemble! 30
How do you, Desdemona?

DESDEMONA   Well, my good lord.

OTHELLO Give me your hand. This hand is moist, my lady.

DESDEMONA It yet hath felt no age, nor known no sorrow.

OTHELLO This argues fruitfulness and liberal heart.
Hot, hot, and moist. This hand of yours requires 35
A sequester from liberty, fasting and prayer,
Much castigation, exercise devout;
For here's a young and sweating devil here
That commonly rebels. 'Tis a good hand,
A frank one.

Othello asks for the handkerchief. When Desdemona denies she has lost it, Othello informs her of its magical powers and its great sentimental value. He claims it was magically made.

1 The myth of the handkerchief (in pairs)

Read Othello's description of the handkerchief's history. It is like a myth or folk tale. Experiment with ways of reading lines 51–71 e.g. as a fairy story for young children.

As a whole class, discuss the significance of the story in the context of the play. Go on to discuss what you understand by the term 'myth' and what part you think myths play in societies in general.

2 What if . . . ? (in groups of three)

What if Desdemona had told Othello the truth at this point, that she had indeed accidentally lost the handkerchief? Each take a part (Desdemona, Emilia, Othello) and speculate how the scene might continue.

Donald Sinden as Othello and Suzanne Bertish as Desdemona in the Royal Shakespeare Company production (1979).

chuck term of endearment	**perdition** damnation
rheum cold	**sibyl** prophetess
charmer witch	**mummy** substance from
amiable beloved	mummified bodies
fancies lovers	

DESDEMONA   You may indeed say so,   40
    For 'twas that hand that gave away my heart.
OTHELLO A liberal hand! The hearts of old gave hands;
    But our new heraldry is hands, not hearts.
DESDEMONA I cannot speak of this. Come now, your promise.
OTHELLO What promise, chuck?   45
DESDEMONA I have sent to bid Cassio come speak with you.
OTHELLO I have a salt and sorry rheum offends me;
    Lend me thy handkerchief.
DESDEMONA   Here, my lord.
OTHELLO That which I gave you.
DESDEMONA   I have it not about me.
OTHELLO Not?   50
DESDEMONA No, faith, my lord.
OTHELLO   That's a fault. That handkerchief
    Did an Egyptian to my mother give:
    She was a charmer and could almost read
    The thoughts of people. She told her, while she kept it,
    'Twould make her amiable and subdue my father   55
    Entirely to her love; but if she lost it
    Or made a gift of it, my father's eye
    Should hold her loathèd and his spirits should hunt
    After new fancies. She dying gave it me,
    And bid me when my fate would have me wive,   60
    To give it her. I did so, and take heed on't:
    Make it a darling, like your precious eye.
    To lose't or give't away were such perdition
    As nothing else could match.
DESDEMONA   Is't possible?
OTHELLO 'Tis true. There's magic in the web of it: 65
    A sibyl, that had numbered in the world
    The sun to course two hundred compasses,
    In her prophetic fury sewed the work;
    The worms were hallowed that did breed the silk,
    And it was dyed in mummy, which the skilful   70
    Conserved of maidens' hearts.

Othello orders Desdemona to bring him the handkerchief. She tries to divert his attention by reminding him of Cassio's unresolved plight, but he leaves, swearing. Emilia comments unflatteringly on men.

1 Desdemona's lie

Write a paragraph explaining what possible reasons there could be for Desdemona telling a very rare lie in the play: 'It is not lost...' (line 79).

2 Men! (in pairs)

Emilia expounds her philosophy concerning men in lines 97–100. Firstly, put her words into modern English. Now attempt to measure her words against various men in the play. In turn take each of the following male characters and formulate what you think their response to such ideas would be:

Othello
Brabantio
Iago
Cassio
Roderigo.

You could try role-playing their responses.

As a whole class discuss men's attitudes to women, then decide whether you think Emilia is justified in her estimation of men.

---

suit original purpose
sufficient competent
Zounds! Gods wounds! (a curse)

DESDEMONA   I'faith, is't true?
OTHELLO Most veritable; therefore look to't well.
DESDEMONA Then would to God that I had never seen't!
OTHELLO Ha? Wherefore?
DESDEMONA Why do you speak so startingly and rash?   75
OTHELLO Is't lost? Is't gone? Speak; is't out of th'way?
DESDEMONA Heaven bless us!
OTHELLO Say you?
DESDEMONA It is not lost, but what and if it were?
OTHELLO How?   80
DESDEMONA I say it is not lost.
OTHELLO   Fetch't, let me see't.
DESDEMONA Why so I can, sir; but I will not now.
      This is a trick to put me from my suit.
      Pray you let Cassio be received again.
OTHELLO Fetch me the handkerchief. My mind misgives.   85
DESDEMONA Come, come;
      You'll never meet a more sufficient man.
OTHELLO The handkerchief!
DESDEMONA   I pray, talk me of Cassio.
OTHELLO The handkerchief!
DESDEMONA   A man that all his time
      Hath founded his good fortunes on your love,   90
      Shared dangers with you –
OTHELLO The handkerchief!
DESDEMONA   I'faith, you are to blame.
OTHELLO Zounds!   *Exit*
EMILIA Is not this man jealous?
DESDEMONA   I ne'er saw this before.
      Sure there's some wonder in this handkerchief;   95
      I am most unhappy in the loss of it.
EMILIA 'Tis not a year or two shows us a man.
      They are all but stomachs, and we all but food;
      They eat us hungerly, and when they are full,
      They belch us.

            Enter IAGO *and* CASSIO.

            Look you, Cassio and my husband.   100
IAGO There is no other way: 'tis she must do't.
      And lo, the happiness! Go, and importune her.

Cassio again asks Desdemona to plead with Othello on his behalf.
She tells him he will have to be patient, since Othello seems to be
behaving strangely. Iago leaves to find Othello.

1 'My lord is not my lord'

Desdemona states in line 118 that Othello is not quite himself. How far would you agree that this is more true than Desdemona realises, in that Othello's identity has been undermined by Iago, who is busily reconstructing a new one for him? Work out your own response to this interpretation, then contribute to a larger group discussion.

2 Intercut (in groups of three)

Look over Iago's short interchange with Emilia and Desdemona (lines 126–34). Both Emilia and Iago know more than they reveal, yet on the surface they appear innocent. Firstly, play with the script, experimenting with ways of acting it out and exploring the undercurrent of (partially) shared knowledge between Emilia and her husband.

Next, attempt to intercut (interweave) script with the unspoken thoughts and preoccupations of the three characters. If, in your initial explorations with acting out the script, you had actors exchanging significant looks, for example, explain in each character's words what is going through their mind at that point. Share your intercut scripts with other groups and discuss any similarities or differences.

---

suit purpose
office loyal service
shut myself up confine myself to
to fortune's alms accepting
  whatever chance may put my way

favour appearance
blank centre of target
of moment momentous

DESDEMONA How now, good Cassio! What's the news with you?

CASSIO Madam, my former suit. I do beseech you
        That, by your virtuous means, I may again   105
        Exist and be a member of his love,
        Whom I, with all the office of my heart,
        Entirely honour. I would not be delayed.
        If my offence be of such mortal kind
        That nor my service past nor present sorrows,   110
        Nor purposed merit in futurity,
        Can ransom me into his love again,
        But to know so must be my benefit:
        So shall I clothe me in a forced content,
        And shut myself up in some other course   115
        To fortune's alms.

DESDEMONA   Alas, thrice-gentle Cassio,
        My advocation is not now in tune:
        My lord is not my lord; nor should I know him,
        Were he in favour as in humour altered.
        So help me every spirit sanctified,   120
        As I have spoken for you all my best,
        And stood within the blank of his displeasure
        For my free speech! You must awhile be patient.
        What I can do, I will; and more I will
        Than for myself I dare. Let that suffice you.   125

IAGO Is my lord angry?

EMILIA   He went hence but now
        And certainly in strange unquietness.

IAGO Can he be angry? I have seen the cannon
        When it hath blown his ranks into the air,
        And like the devil from his very arm   130
        Puffed his own brother – and is he angry?
        Something of moment then. I will go meet him.
        There's matter in't indeed if he be angry.

DESDEMONA I prithee do so.

Exit Iago

Desdemona reassures herself that Othello must be upset by some affair of state. Emilia hopes he is not growing jealous. Desdemona prays he has no such thought in mind and leaves to seek Othello. Bianca comes looking for Cassio.

1 Public and private (in pairs)

In the scenes with Desdemona, it is sometimes easy to forget that Othello's primary role in Cyprus is to administer Venetian rule. In Desdemona's words about 'some unhatched practice' (secret plot or conspiracy), she draws attention to their position as quasi-colonial rulers once again. Discuss what significance this political dimension has for you as you grapple with the 'meaning' of the play.

2 'Men are not gods'

Desdemona assures Cassio and Emilia about this 'fact' – which to you may not seem a particularly earth-shattering revelation for a woman to make. Yet, if you think of gods as being in control of people's lives, as rulers, then might this have some deeper significance in terms of women's role in Venetian society? Is Desdemona's assertion here perhaps a sign that she might be ready to grasp some power and responsibility for herself in her relationship with her husband?

3 Secret thoughts (in groups of three)

(You could extend Activity 2 from the previous page to encompass lines 149–62 of the script from this page.) Try intercutting the script as printed with what you imagine might be the internalised dialogue of the assembled characters.

---

unhatched practice secret conspiracy
endues brings, leads (or infects)
observancy loving attention
bridal wedding night
arraigning accusing

suborned the witness made the witness give false evidence
indicted accused
toy fancy
'Save you God save you: a greeting like 'Hi there!'

                    Something sure of state,
        Either from Venice, or some unhatched practice   135
        Made demonstrable here in Cyprus to him,
        Hath puddled his clear spirit; and in such cases
        Men's natures wrangle with inferior things,
        Though great ones are their object. 'Tis even so;
        For let our finger ache, and it endues   140
        Our other healthful members even to a sense
        Of pain. Nay, we must think men are not gods,
        Nor of them look for such observancy
        As fits the bridal. Beshrew me much, Emilia,
        I was – unhandsome warrior as I am –   145
        Arraigning his unkindness with my soul;
        But now I find I had suborned the witness
        And he's indicted falsely.
EMILIA Pray heaven it be state matters, as you think,
        And no conception nor no jealous toy   150
        Concerning you.
DESDEMONA Alas the day, I never gave him cause.
EMILIA But jealous souls will not be answered so.
        They are not ever jealous for the cause,
        But jealous for they're jealous. 'Tis a monster   155
        Begot upon itself, born on itself.
DESDEMONA Heaven keep that monster from Othello's mind.
EMILIA Lady, amen!
DESDEMONA I will go seek him. Cassio, walk here about.
        If I do find him fit, I'll move your suit   160
        And seek to effect it to my uttermost.
CASSIO I humbly thank your ladyship.
                    Exeunt Desdemona and Emilia

            Enter BIANCA.

BIANCA 'Save you, friend Cassio.
CASSIO   What make you from home?
        How is it with you, my most fair Bianca?
        I'faith, sweet love, I was coming to your house.   165

Bianca accuses Cassio of neglecting her. He pleads that worries have kept him away and gives Bianca the handkerchief, saying he found it in his bedroom. He asks Bianca to leave so that he may meet Othello.

1 Bianca (in groups of three)

What are your first impressions of Bianca, and what relationship do you think she has with Cassio? Explore this question by taking parts. Experiment with ways of playing the script, using your third group member as a director? Which interpretation of Bianca's personality do you prefer?

2 Timing

What is your impression of the amount of time which has elapsed from the beginning of Act 2? From Bianca's words at line 167 it would seem that a whole week has passed by since the Venetian fleet arrived at Cyprus, yet Othello wanted Cassio dead within three days at the end of Scene 3. Many people have tried to sort out the seeming inconsistencies of timing within the play and have written pages on the issue. From your experience as a reader or as a viewer how important do you think such 'textual study' to be?

If Shakespeare is being inconsistent, can you think of reasons for the playwright to do this deliberately?

3 Why?

Why is this little episode with Bianca here? Consider it in terms of plot, themes, dramatic tension, characterisation, politics and relationships. Prepare a short presentation for whole class discussion.

---

continuate uninterrupted
take me this work out copy this
  embroidery for me
be circumstanced put up with

BIANCA   And I was going to your lodging, Cassio.
           What! Keep a week away? Seven days and nights?
           Eight score eight hours? And lovers' absent hours
           More tedious than the dial eight score times!
           O weary reckoning!
CASSIO   Pardon me, Bianca.   170
           I have this while with leaden thoughts been pressed;
           But I shall in a more continuate time
           Strike off this score of absence. Sweet Bianca,
           Take me this work out.
BIANCA   O Cassio, whence came this?
           This is some token from a newer friend.   175
           To the felt absence now I feel a cause.
           Is't come to this? Well, well.
CASSIO   Go to, woman!
           Throw your vile guesses in the devil's teeth
           From whence you have them. You are jealous now
           That this is from some mistress, some remembrance.   180
           No, by my faith, Bianca.
BIANCA   Why, whose is it?
CASSIO   I know not neither; I found it in my chamber.
           I like the work well. Ere it be demanded –
           As like enough it will – I'd have it copied.
           Take it and do't, and leave me for this time.   185
BIANCA   Leave you? Wherefore?
CASSIO   I do attend here on the general;
           And think it no addition, nor my wish,
           To have him see me womaned.
BIANCA   Why, I pray you?
CASSIO   Not that I love you not.
BIANCA   But that you do not love me.   190
           I pray you, bring me on the way a little,
           And say if I shall see you soon at night.
CASSIO   'Tis but a little way that I can bring you,
           For I attend here; but I'll see you soon.
BIANCA   'Tis very good; I must be circumstanced.   195

                          Exeunt

Looking back at Act 3 . . .

1 Iago's tempting (in groups of fifteen to twenty)

Act 3 is the central act of the five act play and is also the longest. At the beginning of Scene 1 Othello is completely in control of himself; by the end of Scene 4 he seems to be verging on insanity. The following activity concentrates on the insidious way in which Iago goes to work on Othello's mind.

Each member of the group should take and learn one of the following lines:

'Ha! I like not that'
'Cassio, my lord? . . . so guilty-like'
'did Michael Cassio . . . know of your love?'
'honest, my lord?'
'I dare be sworn I think that he is honest'
'I perchance am vicious in my guess'
'it is my nature's plague/To spy into abuses'
'I think Cassio's an honest man'
'O beware, my lord, of jealousy'
'Cuckold'
'who dotes yet doubts, suspects, yet fondly loves?'
'the souls of all my tribe defend/From jealousy'
'look to your wife'
'observe her well with Cassio'
'she did deceive her father, marrying you'
'foul disproportion'
'thoughts unnatural'
'note if your lady strain his entertainment'
'behold her topped'
'prime as goats, hot as monkeys'.

Move around the room using all the available space. Try saying your lines out loud in different ways – for example as if you are all spies passing on secrets; small children telling tales; neighbours gossiping.

Next, form a large circle with one student in the centre, blindfolded. Those forming the circle hiss their lines at the central person, perhaps even grabbing hold of her/him and wheeling her/him round as the words are said. Experiment with different ways of presenting your lines, perhaps devising a way of demonstrating the progressive nature of the taunts.

Afterwards, talk together about this group experience. Each person could go on to write a piece entitled 'Honest Iago'.

2 Production photographs

Here are four photographs, each taken during Act 3 and showing Othello and Iago. Can you find an appropriate quotation for each one?

Iago encourages Othello's jealousy with increasingly graphic references to Desdemona's supposed infidelity. He teases Othello with mention of the handkerchief.

1 Opening the scene (in pairs)

Iago's opening words of the scene suggest that he and Othello are part way through a conversation. Speculate what Iago might have been saying before the opening line of script. Role-play the dialogue you create, then read through to line 45.

2 The raven image

In describing his obsession with the lost handkerchief (lines 19–22) Othello uses a simile describing the belief that a croaking raven prophesied death to the inmates of a house, particularly in times of plague. Try creating a graphic design incorporating this image of the bird of ill omen and the handkerchief. It doesn't matter if you don't consider yourself to be much good at art. Ideas are the most important element, not the artist's skills.

venial slip trivial misdeed
importunate suit persistent
chatting-up, wooing

voluntary dotage willing
infatuation
convincèd or supplied
overpowered or seduced

ACT 4   SCENE 1
Cyprus   A room in the castle

Enter OTHELLO *and* IAGO

IAGO Will you think so?

OTHELLO   Think so, Iago?

IAGO   What,
     To kiss in private?

OTHELLO   An unauthorised kiss!

IAGO Or to be naked with her friend in bed
     An hour or more, not meaning any harm?

OTHELLO Naked in bed, Iago, and not mean harm?   5
     It is hypocrisy against the devil.
     They that mean virtuously and yet do so,
     The devil their virtue tempts, and they tempt heaven.

IAGO So they do nothing, 'tis a venial slip;
     But if I give my wife a handkerchief –   10

OTHELLO What then?

IAGO Why, then 'tis hers, my lord; and being hers,
     She may, I think, bestow't on any man.

OTHELLO She is protectress of her honour too.
     May she give that?   15

IAGO Her honour is an essence that's not seen:
     They have it very oft that have it not.
     But for the handkerchief –

OTHELLO By heaven, I would most gladly have forgot it.
     Thou said'st – O it comes o'er my memory,   20
     As doth the raven o'er the infected house,
     Boding to all! – he had my handkerchief.

IAGO Ay, what of that?

OTHELLO   That's not so good now.

IAGO   What
     If I had said I had seen him do you wrong?
     Or heard him say – as knaves be such abroad,   25
     Who having by their own importunate suit
     Or voluntary dotage of some mistress
     Convincèd or supplied them, cannot choose
     But they must blab –

> *Iago implies that Cassio has boasted about having sex with Desdemona.
> Othello is so upset that it appears to bring on an epileptic fit. Cassio
> enters but is persuaded by Iago to leave again.*

1 Othello's fit (in pairs)

What is the effect of Othello's fit on you as a reader or spectator?
Discuss the following views in turn with your partner:

- it makes you wonder just what kind of man is in charge of law and order in Cyprus
- you find it too 'over-the-top' to be believed
- you can enjoy it as pure melodrama
- your sympathy is increased for Othello
- Iago knows exactly where his victim's weak points are
- you admire Iago
- it shows you how much Othello loves Desdemona
- it clearly demonstrates to you how insanely possessive Othello is towards women
- even though Othello is a tough and powerful military leader, it exposes how deeply insecure he is
- his emotional breakdown is not only signalled by the physical 'fit' but is also accompanied by a breakdown in his language
- so much for 'civilised' colonial forces!
- some other responses?

2 Mind and language

To discover something about the state of Othello's mind, read lines
35–41 aloud whilst walking around the room. Change direction
sharply at every punctuation mark. You'll find it's dizzying!

---

belie slander
fulsome revolting
shadowing overwhelming

instruction reason
lethargy loss of consciousness

OTHELLO   Hath he said anything?
IAGO He hath, my lord; but be you well assured   30
          No more than he'll unswear.
OTHELLO   What hath he said?
IAGO Faith, that he did – I know not what he did.
OTHELLO What, what?
IAGO Lie –
OTHELLO   With her?
IAGO   With her, on her, what you will.
OTHELLO Lie with her? Lie on her? We say lie on her when they belie   35
          her. Lie with her! Zounds, that's fulsome! Handkerchief –
          confessions – handkerchief! To confess and be hanged for his
          labour. First to be hanged and then to confess. I tremble at it.
          Nature would not invest herself in such shadowing passion without
          some instruction. It is not words that shakes me thus. Pish! Noses,   40
          ears, and lips. Is't possible? – Confess? Handkerchief? O devil!
                    [*He*] *falls in a trance.*
IAGO Work on,
          My medicine, work! Thus credulous fools are caught;
          And many worthy and chaste dames even thus,
          All guiltless, meet reproach. What ho, my lord!   45
          My lord, I say! Othello!

                    Enter CASSIO.

                    How now, Cassio!
CASSIO What's the matter?
IAGO My lord is fallen into an epilepsy.
          This is his second fit; he had one yesterday.
CASSIO Rub him about the temples.
IAGO   No, forbear.   50
          The lethargy must have his quiet course.
          If not, he foams at mouth and by and by
          Breaks out to savage madness. Look, he stirs.
          Do you withdraw yourself a little while;
          He will recover straight. When he is gone,   55
          I would on great occasion speak with you.
                                        [*Exit Cassio*]

Othello regains consciousness. Iago again assures him of the unfaithfulness of women, then instructs him to eavesdrop on a conversation in which Cassio will tell of his sexual intercourse with Desdemona.

1 'Be a man' (in pairs)

Iago makes four jibes at Othello's 'manhood' in the page of script opposite. Find the four references. Create an improvisation in which you may only use these four 'chunks' of script. Your improvisation need not have anything to do with the plot of *Othello*.

Share your improvisation with other pairs. Afterwards, discuss why Iago chooses to employ such terms of criticism. What is there about Othello (and the society that has formed him) which might make it particularly appropriate?

2 'O thou art wise; 'tis certain' (in groups of three)

Look carefully at Iago's five sentences in lines 63–71. Take each sentence in turn, and talk together about why Othello finds it so persuasive that he replies, 'O, thou art wise'.

3 Husbands and oxen

In lines 64–5, Iago compares husbands to oxen, yoked together to pull ('draw') heavy loads. Make a tableau of this image, or draw it.

4 'Savage madness' (line 53)

Iago is always quick to point out any aspects of Othello's behaviour which conform to a certain racial stereotype. Spend a few moments jotting down the names of characters in the play who stand out in your memory for playing on racist stereotyping. What characters seem to have avoided it so far? Can you begin to draw any conclusions based on these observations?

---

a hornèd man a cuckold: a man thought to have an unfaithful wife was said to grow horns
civil civilised
yoked 'hitched', married
peculiar their own

lip kiss
wanton lecherous person
patient list bounds of patience
ecstasy fit, trance
fleers gibes, mocks and jokes
cope copulate with

How is it, general? Have you not hurt your head?

OTHELLO Dost thou mock me?

IAGO   I mock you? No, by heaven!
Would you would bear your fortune like a man!

OTHELLO A hornèd man's a monster and a beast.   60

IAGO There's many a beast then in a populous city,
And many a civil monster.

OTHELLO Did he confess it?

IAGO   Good sir, be a man:
Think every bearded fellow that's but yoked
May draw with you. There's millions now alive   65
That nightly lie in those unproper beds
Which they dare swear peculiar. Your case is better.
O, 'tis the spite of hell, the fiend's arch-mock,
To lip a wanton in a secure couch
And to suppose her chaste! No, let me know;   70
And knowing what I am, I know what she shall be.

OTHELLO O, thou art wise; 'tis certain.

IAGO   Stand you awhile apart,
Confine yourself but in a patient list.
Whilst you were here, o'erwhelmèd with your grief –
A passion most unsuiting such a man –   75
Cassio came hither. I shifted him away
And laid good scuse upon your ecstasy;
Bade him anon return and here speak with me,
The which he promised. Do but encave yourself,
And mark the fleers, the gibes, and notable scorns   80
That dwell in every region of his face;
For I will make him tell the tale anew,
Where, how, how oft, how long ago, and when
He hath and is again to cope your wife.
I say but mark his gesture. Marry, patience,   85
Or I shall say you're all in all in spleen
And nothing of a man.

OTHELLO   Dost thou hear, Iago?
I will be found most cunning in my patience,
But – dost thou hear – most bloody.

> *Othello hides and Iago reveals he will question Cassio about Bianca.*
> *Othello overhears part of their conversation about Cassio's love life.*
> *He wrongly thinks they speak of Desdemona.*

1 Mime (in groups of three)

Read the page of script, thinking about what movements and gestures would accompany the spoken words. Prepare a version of this eavesdropping episode (starting at line 90), imagining it to be taken from a silent movie. Ensure your gestures are broad and clear, and that characterisation is communicated through the way people move, stand or position themselves.

2 Versions of Bianca

According to Iago, Bianca is a 'housewife' (pronounced 'huzif') or hussey who sells her 'desires' to earn a living. He goes on to make his meaning clearer by calling her a 'strumpet' (a whore). Many editors of *Othello* assume that Bianca is a prostitute, and call her that in the list of characters at the beginning of the playscript. Yet how accurate is Iago as a judge of women? Can we take his description at face value? Flick back through the play reminding yourself of what Iago has said about other women so far.

Next, turn to a partner and compare your findings on Iago's attitude to women. Talk together about what difference it makes to a production of the play if Bianca is quite unequivocally presented as a prostitute. Think about how it reflects on Cassio, and what general image of women is offered through the play given that Bianca represents one third of the women in the cast.

---

unbookish ignorant
construe interpret
addition title
whose want the lack of which
poor caitiff poor thing

Roman like a victorious Roman warrior
customer whore
bear some charity give some credit

IAGO   That's not amiss.
         But yet keep time in all. Will you withdraw?   90
                  [*Othello withdraws.*]
         Now will I question Cassio of Bianca,
         A housewife that by selling her desires
         Buys herself bread and clothes. It is a creature
         That dotes on Cassio; as 'tis the strumpet's plague
         To beguile many and be beguiled by one.   95
         He, when he hears of her, cannot refrain
         From the excess of laughter. Here he comes.

                  Enter Cassio.

         As he shall smile, Othello shall go mad;
         And his unbookish jealousy must construe
         Poor Cassio's smiles, gestures, and light behaviours   100
         Quite in the wrong. How do you now, lieutenant?
CASSIO The worser that you give me the addition
         Whose want even kills me.
IAGO Ply Desdemona well and you are sure on't.
         Now if this suit lay in Bianca's power,   105
         How quickly should you speed!
CASSIO   Alas, poor caitiff!
OTHELLO [*Aside*] Look how he laughs already!
IAGO I never knew a woman love man so.
CASSIO Alas, poor rogue! I think, i'faith, she loves me.
OTHELLO [*Aside*] Now he denies it faintly, and laughs it out.   110
IAGO Do you hear, Cassio?
OTHELLO [*Aside*]   Now he importunes him
         To tell it o'er. Go to, well said, well said!
IAGO She gives it out that you shall marry her.
         Do you intend it?
CASSIO Ha, ha, ha!   115
OTHELLO [*Aside*] Do you triumph, Roman? Do you triumph?
CASSIO I marry her? What! A customer! I prithee, bear some
         charity to my wit. Do not think it so unwholesome. Ha, ha, ha!
OTHELLO [*Aside*] So, so, so, so: they laugh that wins.

*Othello continues to believe wrongly that Cassio speaks of Desdemona.
He watches as Bianca meets Cassio and flings the handkerchief back in
his face, supposing it had been given him by some other woman.*

1 How to condition someone's response

Iago has conditioned Othello's response to Cassio's behaviour
through careful preparation (see his words at lines 79–85). Othello
has chosen one particular interpretation of what he has seen and
heard first hand: his version of the 'truth'.

Our interpretation of an event, a photograph, or a political situation
is shaped by the context in which it happens, or in which we exist. For
example, our response to a bus-drivers' strike would be conditioned
by our relationship to it: whether we were a bus-driver, a passenger or
the owner of the bus company. Our response may be further
conditioned by our choice of newspaper and other sources of
information.

As a simple classroom experiment in conditioning someone's
perception, make three 'flash cards' as follows:

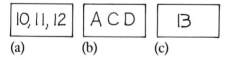

(a)   (b)   (c)

Show one group of people card (a), and show a separate group card
(b). Don't let either group see the other card. Now show both groups
card (c) and ask them to write down what they see. It is likely that the
majority of the first group will see a B, and the second will interpret it
as a 13. You can try the same experiment using 'IV' on the third card,
with I, II, III/ IR, IS, IT on the other two cards.

Talk together about how this experiment helps you understand
Othello's responses and how skilfully Iago goes about his task.

---

scored wounded
bauble pretty thing
hales tugs

such another fitchew none other
  than that polecat
Marry By Mary (a mild oath)
hobby-horse whore

IAGO Faith, the cry goes that you shall marry her.   120
CASSIO Prithee, say true.
IAGO I am a very villain else.
OTHELLO [*Aside*] Have you scored me? Well.
CASSIO This is the monkey's own giving out. She is persuaded I will
    marry her out of her own love and flattery, not out of my   125
    promise.
OTHELLO [*Aside*] Iago beckons me. Now he begins the story.
CASSIO She was here even now. She haunts me in every place. I was
    the other day talking on the sea-bank with certain Venetians, and
    thither comes this bauble and, by this hand, falls me thus   130
    about my neck.
OTHELLO [*Aside*] Crying 'O dear Cassio!' as it were. His gesture
    imports it.
CASSIO So hangs and lolls and weeps upon me, so hales and pulls me.
    Ha, ha, ha!   135
OTHELLO [*Aside*] Now he tells how she plucked him to my chamber.
    O, I see that nose of yours, but not that dog I shall throw it
    to!
CASSIO Well, I must leave her company.
IAGO Before me, look where she comes!   140
CASSIO 'Tis such another fitchew! Marry, a perfumed one.

              Enter BIANCA.

    What do you mean by this haunting of me?
BIANCA Let the devil and his dam haunt you! What did you mean
    by that same handkerchief you gave me even now? I was a fine fool
    to take it. I must take out the work? A likely piece of work   145
    that you should find it in your chamber and not know who left
    it there! This is some minx's token, and I must take out the work?
    There, give it your hobby-horse, wheresoever you had it. I'll
    take out no work on't.
CASSIO How now, my sweet Bianca! How now, how now!   150
OTHELLO [*Aside*] By heaven, that should be my handkerchief!
BIANCA If you'll come to supper tonight, you may. If you will not,
    come when you are next prepared for.   *Exit*

Cassio leaves to prevent further outbursts by Bianca. Othello determines to kill both Cassio and Desdemona, but is torn between violent hatred and love for his wife. Iago persuades him to put aside any remaining affection.

---

1 'How shall I murder him?'

These words constitute Othello's immediate reaction to the dialogue he has just overheard at line 162. As a reader or spectator, are you shocked by the brutality of the words? Write a paragraph trying to account for Othello's response. For example, would you say it's understandable because Othello is a professional soldier, a man used to fighting?

2 In action (in groups of three)

Explore different ways of reading lines 162–200, for example, whispering, ranting, reasoning, etc.

Experiment with movement and positioning:

- using two group members as Othello, and the third as Iago, sharing Othello's lines according to the mood and attitude they reflect.
- standing back-to-back
- moving constantly around the room
- staying in the same place
- having Iago always behind Othello, whispering in his ear.

3 'The pity of it, Iago!'

Do you think Iago could ever feel pity?

---

rail shout
by this hand I swear it
a-killing dying a slow death

fond over foolish about
patent licence

IAGO After her, after her!

CASSIO Faith, I must. She'll rail in the streets else.   155

IAGO Will you sup there?

CASSIO Faith, I intend so.

IAGO Well, I may chance to see you; for I would very fain speak with
you.

CASSIO Prithee, come; will you?   160

IAGO Go to; say no more.

Exit Cassio

OTHELLO [*Coming forward.*] How shall I murder him, Iago?

IAGO Did you perceive how he laughed at his vice?

OTHELLO O, Iago!

IAGO And did you see the handkerchief?   165

OTHELLO Was that mine?

IAGO Yours, by this hand. And to see how he prizes the foolish woman
your wife: she gave it him, and he hath given it his whore.

OTHELLO I would have him nine years a-killing. A fine woman, a fair
woman, a sweet woman!   170

IAGO Nay, you must forget that.

OTHELLO Ay, let her rot and perish, and be damned tonight, for she
shall not live. No, my heart is turned to stone: I strike it and it
hurts my hand. O, the world hath not a sweeter creature! She
might lie by an emperor's side and command him tasks.   175

IAGO Nay, that's not your way.

OTHELLO Hang her, I do but say what she is: so delicate with her needle,
an admirable musician – O, she will sing the savageness out of a
bear – of so high and plenteous wit and invention –

IAGO She's the worse for all this.   180

OTHELLO O, a thousand, thousand times – and then of so gentle
a condition!

IAGO Ay, too gentle.

OTHELLO Nay, that's certain; but yet the pity of it, Iago! O Iago,
the pity of it, Iago!   185

IAGO If you are so fond over her iniquity, give her patent to offend;
for if it touch not you, it comes near nobody.

OTHELLO I will chop her into messes. Cuckold me!

IAGO O, 'tis foul in her.

OTHELLO With mine officer!   190

IAGO That's fouler.

Othello determines to follow Iago's suggestion to strangle Desdemona in her bed. Iago promises to kill Cassio that night. Lodovico brings Othello a letter from Venice and asks about Cassio.

1 'Justice'

According to Othello, to strangle his wife in bed represents 'justice' (line 197). Justice can, therefore, be added to a growing list of words which have been redefined in the course of the play. For an activity on redefined terms in the play as a whole, see page 182.

2 Lodovico (in pairs)

Outline how you would stage Lodovico's entrance if you were directing a production of the play. Work out who would accompany Lodovico, and how they would be dressed. Decide on the advice you would give an actor playing Lodovico regarding his tone, manner and general bearing. How would you justify your decisions?

3 Two words (in small groups)

Tiny sections of a play can be highly charged with significance. At line 212, Iago says only 'Lives, sir'. But *how* does he say it, and how does Lodovico (and everyone else) react? Talk together about whether the remark is in character for Iago.

expostulate discuss
unprovide weaken
in the paper reading the letter

OTHELLO Get me some poison, Iago, this night. I'll not expostulate
    with her, lest her body and beauty unprovide my mind again – this
    night, Iago.
IAGO Do it not with poison; strangle her in her bed, even the bed she   195
    hath contaminated.
OTHELLO Good, good! The justice of it pleases; very good!
IAGO And for Cassio, let me be his undertaker. You shall hear more
    by midnight.
OTHELLO Excellent good!   200
                        A trumpet [sounds within].
    What trumpet is that same?
IAGO I warrant something from Venice.

                Enter LODOVICO, DESDEMONA *and* ATTENDANTS.

    'Tis Lodovico. This comes from the duke. See, your wife's with
    him.
LODOVICO God save you, worthy general!
OTHELLO   With all my heart, sir.   205
LODOVICO The duke and senators of Venice greet you.
                    [*He gives Othello a letter.*]
OTHELLO I kiss the instrument of their pleasures.
                    [*He opens the letter and reads.*]
DESDEMONA And what's the news, good cousin Lodovico?
IAGO I am very glad to see you, signior;
    Welcome to Cyprus.   210
LODOVICO I thank you. How does Lieutenant Cassio?
IAGO Lives, sir.
DESDEMONA Cousin, there's fallen between him and my lord
    An unkind breach; but you shall make all well.
OTHELLO Are you sure of that?   215
DESDEMONA My lord?
OTHELLO 'This fail you not to do, as you will –'
LODOVICO He did not call; he's busy in the paper.
    Is there division 'twixt my lord and Cassio?
DESDEMONA A most unhappy one; I would do much   220
    T'atone them, for the love I bear to Cassio.
OTHELLO Fire and brimstone!
DESDEMONA My lord?

Lodovico reveals that the letter orders Othello to be recalled to Venice and Cassio made governor of Cyprus. Desdemona says she is pleased. Othello strikes her in front of the Venetian delegation, and rages at her.

1 The Duke's letter

The Duke's decision to recall Othello, 'deputing Cassio in his government' elicits Desdemona's response: 'By my troth, I am glad on't.' As a reader or listener what is *your* response to the news? Can you predict any possible outcome(s) of this promised change?

2 The physical blow (in pairs)

Othello striking Desdemona openly on stage was thought by some nineteenth-century directors to be too shocking to show, consequently they omitted it. Talk together about what difference it would make to a production if that act of violence were missed out. Would you retain it?

3 Show the moment (in groups of five or six)

Create a tableau (a 'freeze-frame') of the action at line 231: 'I have not deserved this.' Make sure that characters are recognisable from their reactions, their spatial relationships and their frozen gestures. Show your tableau to the rest of the class for them to guess who the different characters are. To add an extra layer of sophistication to your work, ask individual characters to step out of the freeze-frame and explain what is going through their mind at that moment.

4 Othello's syntax (in groups of three)

Look carefully at Othello's syntax (sentence structure) in lines 243–54. What is different about his way of speaking here in comparison with his early speeches (for example, 1.3.127–69)? By exploring different ways of speaking the lines, discuss what they tell you about his state of mind. Write two paragraphs on Othello's changed language.

---

mistress term used to address a prostitute in a brothel
mandate command

avaunt get out of my sight
goats and monkeys supposedly lecherous beasts

OTHELLO Are you wise?

DESDEMONA What, is he angry?

LODOVICO   Maybe the letter moved him;   225
    For as I think they do command him home,
    Deputing Cassio in his government.

DESDEMONA By my troth, I am glad on't.

OTHELLO   Indeed!

DESDEMONA   My lord?

OTHELLO I am glad to see you mad.

DESDEMONA   Why, sweet Othello?

OTHELLO Devil!   230

                     [He strikes her.]

DESDEMONA I have not deserved this.

LODOVICO My lord, this would not be believed in Venice,
    Though I should swear I saw't. 'Tis very much.
    Make her amends; she weeps.

OTHELLO   O devil, devil!
    If that the earth could teem with woman's tears,   235
    Each drop she falls would prove a crocodile.
    Out of my sight!

DESDEMONA   I will not stay to offend you.

LODOVICO Truly, an obedient lady.
    I do beseech your lordship, call her back.

OTHELLO Mistress!   240

DESDEMONA My lord?

OTHELLO What would you with her, sir?

LODOVICO   Who? I, my lord?

OTHELLO Ay, you did wish that I would make her turn.
    Sir, she can turn, and turn, and yet go on,
    And turn again. And she can weep, sir, weep.   245
    And she's obedient; as you say, obedient,
    Very obedient – proceed you in your tears –
    Concerning this, sir, – O, well-painted passion! –
    I am commanded home – get you away!
    I'll send for you anon. – Sir, I obey the mandate,   250
    And will return to Venice. – Hence, avaunt!
                       [Exit Desdemona]
    Cassio shall have my place. And, sir, tonight
    I do entreat that we may sup together.
    You are welcome, sir, to Cyprus. Goats and monkeys! *Exit*

Lodovico expresses his horror to Iago of what he has just seen. Iago remarks that Othello is greatly changed. The next scene opens with Othello questioning Emilia about his wife's infidelity.

1 The man 'whom passion could not shake' (in pairs)

Discuss whether you consider a lack of emotion in a man to be an admirable quality or not. Relate your discussion to Othello. What does it say about Venetian society that such a lack of emotion was greatly valued in a leader?

2 Iago's persuasive skill

Some readers of the play have stressed Othello's stupidity and gullibility in being taken in by Iago. However, it is testimony to Iago's acting skill that he has succeeded in convincing everyone, including Lodovico at this point. Lodovico says with heavy (unconscious) irony: 'I am sorry that I am deceived in him' (meaning Othello). Examine each of Iago's comments to Lodovico and assess his skill in the way he imparts an opinion without seeming to do so.

3 Imagine the scene (in groups of three)

Imagine Lodovico and two other members of his delegation later on that day, talking about what they had seen when they delivered the Duke's letter to Othello. Take roles and improvise the scene as they relax in a private room together.

---

all-in-all sufficient fully
  competent
censure judgement
use custom

LODOVICO Is this the noble Moor whom our full senate   255
          Call all-in-all sufficient? Is this the nature
          Whom passion could not shake? Whose solid virtue
          The shot of accident nor dart of chance
          Could neither graze nor pierce?
IAGO   He is much changed.
LODOVICO Are his wits safe? Is he not light of brain?   260
IAGO He's that he is; I may not breathe my censure
          What he might be. If what he might he is not,
          I would to heaven he were.
LODOVICO   What! Strike his wife!
IAGO Faith, that was not so well; yet would I knew
          That stroke would prove the worst.
LODOVICO   Is it his use?   265
          Or did the letters work upon his blood
          And new-create this fault?
IAGO   Alas, alas!
          It is not honesty in me to speak
          What I have seen and known. You shall observe him,
          And his own courses will denote him so,
          That I may save my speech. Do but go after,   270
          And mark how he continues.
LODOVICO I am sorry that I am deceived in him.

                                        Exeunt

ACT 4   SCENE 2
Cyprus   Another room in the castle

Enter OTHELLO and EMILIA

OTHELLO You have seen nothing then?
EMILIA Nor ever heard, nor ever did suspect.
OTHELLO Yes, you have seen Cassio and she together.
EMILIA But then I saw no harm, and then I heard
          Each syllable that breath made up between them.   5

Emilia states categorically that Desdemona is innocent. Othello sends for his wife. He dismisses Emilia, treating her as a brothel-keeper.

1 Key words (in groups of three)

Emilia 'durst . . . wager' (swear) that Desdemona is 'honest'. Unfortunately, that word has become redefined in the course of the play, and appropriated exclusively by Iago.

Take lines 11–22 and choose one key word from each line. Spend some time discussing what each of you think to be key words.

Next, find ways of presenting the key words in a dramatically appropriate way: mime, stylised movement, a series of tableaux, choral speech or a short play.

2 Improvise an image

Othello uses the image of 'a closet lock and key of villainous secrets' (a cupboard securely locked) in reference to Desdemona.

Either:

a in groups of between three and five, build an improvisation around the image

or:

b on your own, create a design to illustrate the image. Make it poster sized for display on your classroom wall.

3 How does she act? (in pairs)

Decide how Desdemona would behave and sound on the words 'My lord, what is your will?' (line 23). Experiment, then make a directorial decision. Be prepared to justify it to the rest of the class.

---

durst dare
bawd brothel-keeper
some of your function get on with
   your job (as brothel-keeper)

procreants those engaged in sex
your mystery get on with your
   trade

OTHELLO What! Did they never whisper?
EMILIA   Never, my lord.
OTHELLO Nor send you out o'th'way?
EMILIA   Never.
OTHELLO To fetch her fan, her gloves, her mask, nor nothing?
EMILIA Never, my lord.
OTHELLO That's strange.   10
EMILIA I durst, my lord, to wager she is honest,
        Lay down my soul at stake. If you think other,
        Remove your thought; it doth abuse your bosom.
        If any wretch have put this in your head,
        Let heaven requite it with the serpent's curse!   15
        For if she be not honest, chaste, and true,
        There's no man happy. The purest of their wives
        Is foul as slander.
OTHELLO   Bid her come hither; go!

Exit Emilia

        She says enough; yet she's a simple bawd
        That cannot say as much. This is a subtle whore,   20
        A closet lock and key of villainous secrets;
        And yet she'll kneel and pray. I have seen her do't.

Enter DESDEMONA *and Emilia.*

DESDEMONA My lord, what is your will?
OTHELLO   Pray, chuck, come hither.
DESDEMONA What is your pleasure?
OTHELLO   Let me see your eyes.
        Look in my face.
DESDEMONA   What horrible fancy's this?   25
OTHELLO [*To Emilia*] Some of your function, mistress:
        Leave procreants alone and shut the door;
        Cough or cry 'hem' if anybody come.
        Your mystery, your mystery! Nay, dispatch!

Exit Emilia

DESDEMONA Upon my knees, what doth your speech import?   30
        I understand a fury in your words,
        But not the words.
OTHELLO   Why? What art thou?

163

Othello accuses Desdemona of gross dishonesty. She doesn't understand what he is talking about, but thinks his anger may be because he has been recalled to Venice by Brabantio's plotting.

1 Why? (in pairs)

Spend five minutes discussing why you think Othello avoids answering Desdemona's direct questions: 'To whom? . . . With whom? How . . . ?' (line 39).

2 Nature in Othello's language (in groups of three)

Read through Othello's lines 46–68. As one person reads, the other two echo any words or phrases connected with nature, for example, images of beauty or decay.

Next, go through the speeches in more detail, picking out all the references to nature that you can discover. Divide them up between the group members according to broadly similar types of image. Explore ways of presenting your new 'script' in an appropriate way.

Show your presentation to the rest of the class, then discuss how helpful this exercise has been in allowing you further insights into Othello's language and mind.

3 Draw the image

Study lines 53–4 and design the image it suggests: is it a clock, a statue, or something else?

---

lost him lost his favour
garnered up my heart stored up
  my love
gender breed
cherubin angel

shambles slaughterhouses
quicken even with blowing hatch
  as soon as the eggs are laid
ignorant unknowing

DESDEMONA Your wife, my lord; your true and loyal wife.

OTHELLO Come, swear it; damn thyself;

        Lest, being like one of heaven, the devils themselves   35

        Should fear to seize thee. Therefore be double-damned:

        Swear thou art honest.

DESDEMONA   Heaven doth truly know it.

OTHELLO Heaven truly knows that thou art false as hell.

DESDEMONA To whom, my lord? With whom? How am I false?

OTHELLO Ah, Desdemon, away, away, away!   40

DESDEMONA Alas, the heavy day! Why do you weep?

        Am I the motive of these tears, my lord?

        If haply you my father do suspect

        An instrument of this your calling back,

        Lay not your blame on me. If you have lost him,   45

        I have lost him too.

OTHELLO   Had it pleased heaven

        To try me with affliction, had they rained

        All kind of sores and shames on my bare head,

        Steeped me in poverty to the very lips,

        Given to captivity me and my utmost hopes,   50

        I should have found in some place of my soul

        A drop of patience. But, alas, to make me

        The fixèd figure for the time of scorn

        To point his slow unmoving finger at!

        Yet could I bear that too, well, very well;   55

        But there where I have garnered up my heart,

        Where either I must live or bear no life,

        The fountain from the which my current runs

        Or else dries up – to be discarded thence

        Or keep it as a cistern for foul toads   60

        To knot and gender in! Turn thy complexion there,

        Patience, thou young and rose-lipped cherubin;

        Ay, there look grim as hell!

DESDEMONA I hope my noble lord esteems me honest.

OTHELLO O ay: as summer flies are in the shambles,   65

        That quicken even with blowing. O, thou weed,

        Who art so lovely fair and smell'st so sweet

        That the sense aches at thee, would thou hadst ne'er been

        born!

DESDEMONA Alas, what ignorant sin have I committed?

> *Othello calls Desdemona a whore to her face. He, ignores her pleas of innocence, and continues to treat Emilia and Desdemona as if they work in a brothel.*

1 Cosmic images (in pairs)

Othello uses imagery of the heavens in his answer to Desdemona's innocent question, 'what ignorant sin have I committed?' (line 69). He states that 'heaven stops the nose at it' (the smell of Desdemona's sin), 'the moon winks' (the moon refuses to look) and 'The bawdy wind, that kisses all it meets, is hushed within the hollow mine of earth and will not hear it' (lines 76–9). So, her sin is so revolting and so wide-reaching that heaven, moon and wind are unable to bear it. You may feel that this is a gross exaggeration if taken literally. But what does it indicate about Othello's state of mind and how he interprets his wife's behaviour? Discuss this with a partner after re-reading the lines.

2 Emilia's version (in pairs)

In his last two encounters with Emilia, Othello has persisted in addressing her as if she's a 'madam' and Desdemona is one of her working prostitutes. At line 92 he tells Emilia, 'We have done our course' (finished our business) and then proceeds to pay her! Imagine what Emilia might say about all of this to a friend amongst the other 'army wives'. Build up an improvisation based on an imaginary scene where Emilia confides in a friend and gives her version of all that has happened so far since their arrival in Cyprus.

3 Othello's questions (in groups of four)

Read through Othello's part opposite and note all the questions he asks. Match Desdemona's reply with each question, where appropriate. Compile a list of these questions and answers.

Work out an active and dramatic way of presenting the questions and answers.

Saint Peter the saint who guards
the gates of heaven
conceive imagine

OTHELLO Was this fair paper, this most goodly book,   70
       Made to write 'whore' upon? What committed!
       Committed? O thou public commoner!
       I should make very forges of my cheeks
       That would to cinders burn up modesty
       Did I but speak thy deeds. What committed!   75
       Heaven stops the nose at it, and the moon winks;
       The bawdy wind, that kisses all it meets,
       Is hushed within the hollow mine of earth
       And will not hear it. What committed?
       Impudent strumpet!
DESDEMONA   By heaven, you do me wrong.   80
OTHELLO Are not you a strumpet?
DESDEMONA   No, as I am a Christian.
       If to preserve this vessel for my lord
       From any other foul unlawful touch
       Be not to be a strumpet, I am none.
OTHELLO What, not a whore?
DESDEMONA   No, as I shall be saved.   85
OTHELLO Is't possible?
DESDEMONA O, heaven forgive us!
OTHELLO   I cry you mercy then:
       I took you for that cunning whore of Venice
       That married with Othello. You, mistress,
       That have the office opposite to Saint Peter,   90
       And keeps the gate of hell! You, you, ay, you!

Enter Emilia.

       We have done our course; there's money for your pains.
       I pray you turn the key, and keep our counsel.   *Exit*
EMILIA Alas, what does this gentleman conceive?
       How do you, madam? How do you, my good lady?   95
DESDEMONA Faith, half-asleep.
EMILIA Good madam, what's the matter with my lord?
DESDEMONA With who?
EMILIA Why, with my lord, madam.
DESDEMONA Who is thy lord?
EMILIA   He that is yours, sweet lady.   100

Desdemona expresses her distress and bewilderment at Othello's treatment of her. She cannot speak the word 'whore'. Emilia speculates it is all the trick of a villain seeking promotion.

---

1 Desdemona's response (in pairs or groups of three)

Many modern readers of the play have found Desdemona's utter submissiveness in the face of severe provocation rather frustrating. However, it is also argued that her behaviour might have been regarded by some people in the past as exemplary for a married woman. How would you act if you were a woman faced with similar circumstances? Put your 'wedding sheets' on the bed and hope for the best? Or pack your bags and slam a few doors on the way out? Discuss what courses of action you would take yourselves. Then look particularly at the precise social constraints operating on Desdemona. What options are realistically open to her in the society in which she lives?

2 'Some eternal villain . . .' (in pairs)

Emilia's guess that 'some eternal villain . . .' is responsible for the 'slander' (lines 129–32) is extremely accurate. The dramatic irony is made even more acute by the fact that Iago is present. Has Emilia realised the truth? Do you believe her words contain a guarded warning, or is it just a case of unconscious irony? Discuss with your partner, then try to predict how Iago will react on stage, and what reply (if any) Iago might make – don't turn the page until you've both had a guess!

---

should go by water be expressed in tears
meet fitting, appropriate
a child to chiding not used to being verbally abused

callet slut
cogging, cozening cheating, deceiving
office job

Act 4 Scene 2

DESDEMONA I have none. Do not talk to me, Emilia.
        I cannot weep, nor answers have I none
        But what should go by water. Prithee tonight
        Lay on my bed my wedding sheets, remember;
        And call thy husband hither.
EMILIA   Here's a change indeed! *Exit* 105
DESDEMONA 'Tis meet I should be used so, very meet!
        How have I been behaved that he might stick
        The smallest opinion on my least misuse?

        Enter IAGO and Emilia.

IAGO What is your pleasure, madam? How is't with you?
DESDEMONA I cannot tell. Those that do teach young babes 110
        Do it with gentle means and easy tasks.
        He might have chid me so; for, in good faith,
        I am a child to chiding.
IAGO   What is the matter, lady?
EMILIA Alas, Iago, my lord hath so bewhored her,
        Thrown such despite and heavy terms upon her 115
        As true hearts cannot bear.
DESDEMONA Am I that name, Iago?
IAGO   What name, fair lady?
DESDEMONA Such as she said my lord did say I was.
EMILIA He called her whore. A beggar in his drink
        Could not have laid such terms upon his callet. 120
IAGO Why did he so?
DESDEMONA I do not know; I am sure I am none such.
IAGO Do not weep, do not weep! Alas the day!
EMILIA Hath she forsook so many noble matches,
        Her father, and her country, and her friends,
        To be called whore? Would it not make one weep? 125
DESDEMONA It is my wretched fortune.
IAGO   Beshrew him for't!
        How comes this trick upon him?
DESDEMONA   Nay, heaven doth know.
EMILIA I will be hanged if some eternal villain,
        Some busy and insinuating rogue,
        Some cogging, cozening slave, to get some office, 130
        Have not devised this slander; I'll be hanged else.

169

Emilia continues to suggest that a villain has poisoned Othello's mind. She reminds Iago that he has suspected her of infidelity with Othello. Desdemona professes her undying love for Othello whatever happens.

1 'Some most villainous knave' (in groups of three)

Emilia continues her railing against the 'scurvy fellow' who might be at the back of Othello's uncharacteristic behaviour. Look carefully at Iago's spoken replies. We can't tell from the words alone whether he is nervously alert, dangerously threatening towards Emilia, or confident that he remains undiscovered. Starting with Emilia's 'I will be hanged' (line 129), experiment with different ways of acting out the script down to line 147.

2 Iago's secret thoughts (in pairs)

Work on Desdemona's lines 147–63. Break up the speech into meaningful units (phrases, lines, sentences) and punctuate Desdemona's words with Iago's undisclosed thoughts. Present your version of this 'intercutting' activity to the rest of the class.

famous line about Iago

"motiveless malignity"

no reasons for his behavior seem to be (valid)

---

halter noose
within door quietly
seamy side without inside out

2 DIFFERENT REACTIONS (handwritten)

wedding (ring) closed? (handwritten)

IAGO Fie, there is no such man; it is impossible.

→ No-one would be so mean (handwritten)

DESDEMONA If any such there be, heaven pardon him.

I would forgive (handwritten)

EMILIA A halter pardon him and hell gnaw his bones!   135
    Why should he call her whore? Who keeps her company?

stands up (handwritten)

    What place, what time, what form, what likelihood?
    The Moor's abused by some most villainous knave,
    Some base notorious knave, some scurvy fellow.

quite convinced it's made up (handwritten)

    O heaven, that such companions thou'dst unfold,   140
    And put in every honest hand a whip
    To lash the rascals naked through the world,
    Even from the east to th'west!

IAGO   Speak within door.

→ shut up. (handwritten)

EMILIA O fie upon them! Some such squire he was
    That turned your wit the seamy side without   145
    And made you to suspect me with the Moor.

→ look back. (handwritten)

IAGO You are a fool, go to.

DESDEMONA   O good Iago,
    What shall I do to win my lord again?
    Good friend, go to him; for, by this light of heaven,
    I know not how I lost him. Here I kneel: 150
    If e'er my will did trespass 'gainst his love
    Either in discourse of thought or actual deed;
    Or that mine eyes, mine ears, or any sense
    Delighted them in any other form;
    Or that I do not yet, and ever did,
    And ever will – though he do shake me off   155
    To beggarly divorcement – love him dearly,
    Comfort forswear me! Unkindness may do much,
    And his unkindness may defeat my life,
    But never taint my love. I cannot say 'whore':   160
    It does abhor me now I speak the word;
    To do the act that might the addition earn
    Not the world's mass of vanity could make me.

I WILL STILL LOVE HIM (handwritten)

IAGO I pray you be content; 'tis but his humour.
    The business of the state does him offence,   165
    And he does chide with you.

DESDEMONA If 'twere no other –

IAGO   It is but so, I warrant.

Emilia and Desdemona go off to dinner with the Venetian visitors.
Roderigo expresses his disgruntlement and accuses Iago of tricking him
out of jewellery intended to be passed on to Desdemona. He threatens Iago.

1 What happened at dinner? (in groups of six or seven)

After the highly emotional episode of marital strife, Desdemona is
called to a formal dinner to entertain her Venetian guests. This is not
a scene which Shakespeare chose to stage, but there are strong
dramatic possibilities in such an artificially polite and formal occasion,
with its seething undercurrents of highly charged emotional discord.
Improvise the imagined scene, giving due consideration to how
Othello, Desdemona, Emilia and Lodovico might speak and behave
towards one another in public.

2 How should it be played? (in pairs)

The episode between Iago and Roderigo has been differently interpreted by readers and directors. Some see it as continuing to raise the
tension. Others see it as having strong comic possibilities through the
character of Roderigo, and thereby lowering the tension briefly. Read
lines 171–235 aloud to each other, then discuss how you would play
the scene, giving your reasons.

stay the meat await the meal
daff'st me fob me off
votarist nun

sudden respect immediate
  attention
fopped fooled
seek satisfaction challenge to a
  duel

[*Trumpets sound within.*]
Hark how these instruments summon to supper!
The messengers of Venice stay the meat.
Go in, and weep not; all things shall be well.   170
                              Exeunt Desdemona and Emilia

Enter RODERIGO.

How now, Roderigo?
RODERIGO I do not find that thou deal'st justly with me.
IAGO What in the contrary?
RODERIGO Every day thou daff'st me with some device, Iago, and
   rather, as it seems to me now, keep'st from me all conveniency   175
   than suppliest me with the least advantage of hope. I will indeed
   no longer endure it. Nor am I yet persuaded to put up in peace
   what already I have foolishly suffered.
IAGO Will you hear me, Roderigo?
RODERIGO Faith, I have heard too much; for your words and   180
   performances are no kin together.
IAGO You charge me most unjustly.
RODERIGO With naught but truth. I have wasted myself out of my
   means. The jewels you have had from me to deliver to Desdemona
   would half have corrupted a votarist. You have told me she hath   185
   received them, and returned me expectations and comforts of
   sudden respect and acquaintance, but I find none.
IAGO Well, go to; very well.
RODERIGO Very well, go to! I cannot go to, man, nor 'tis not very
   well. By this hand, I say 'tis very scurvy and begin to find myself 190
   fopped in it.
IAGO Very well.
RODERIGO I tell you 'tis not very well. I will make myself known to
   Desdemona. If she will return me my jewels, I will give over my
   suit and repent my unlawful solicitation; if not, assure yourself I   195
   will seek satisfaction of you.
IAGO You have said now?

Iago promises Roderigo that Desdemona will be available for him soon. He plots that Roderigo shall kill Cassio that night as Cassio leaves Bianca's house.

IAGO IS IN DRIVING SEAT.

RODERIGO IS UPSET.

Iago and Roderigo, Royal Shakespeare Company (1989).

engines for plots against
Mauritania a region of North Africa
abode be lingered stay be prolonged

harlotry harlot → prostitute
second support
necessity in need for
put it on him kill him

RODERIGO Ay, and said nothing but what I protest intendment of
     doing.

IAGO Why, now I see there's mettle in thee, and even from this instant   200
     do build on thee a better opinion than ever before. Give me thy
     hand, Roderigo. Thou hast taken against me a most just
     exception; but yet I protest I have dealt most directly in thy
     affair.

RODERIGO It hath not appeared.   205

IAGO I grant indeed it hath not appeared; and your suspicion is not
     without wit and judgement. But, Roderigo, if thou hast that in
     thee indeed, which I have greater reason to believe now than ever – I
     mean purpose, courage, and valour – this night show it. If thou the
     next night following enjoy not Desdemona, take me from this   210
     world with treachery, and devise engines for my life.

RODERIGO Well, what is it? Is it within reason and compass?

IAGO Sir, there is especial commission come from Venice to depute
     Cassio in Othello's place.

RODERIGO Is that true? Why, then Othello and Desdemona return again   215
     to Venice.

IAGO O no, he goes into Mauritania and takes away with him the
     fair Desdemona, unless his abode be lingered here by some
     accident; wherein none can be so determinate as the removing of
     Cassio.   220

RODERIGO How do you mean 'removing' of him?

IAGO Why, by making him uncapable of Othello's place – knocking out
     his brains.

RODERIGO And that you would have me to do?

IAGO Ay, if you dare do yourself a profit and a right. He sups tonight   225
     with a harlotry, and thither will I go to him. He knows not yet of
     his honourable fortune. If you will watch his going thence – which
     I will fashion to fall out between twelve and one – you may take
     him at your pleasure. I will be near to second your attempt, and
     he shall fall between us. Come, stand not amazed at it, but go along 230
     with me. I will show you such a necessity in his death that you shall
     think yourself bound to put it on him. It is now high supper-time
     and the night grows to waste. About it!

RODERIGO I will hear further reason for this.

IAGO And you shall be satisfied.   235

                                                        Exeunt

Othello bids goodnight to Lodovico after their dinner, and orders Desdemona to go to bed to await him. She talks with Emilia of her love for Othello, of death, and of Barbary, her mother's maid.

1 Polite forms of address (in groups of three or four)

Read through the script up to Othello's exit at line 9. The dialogue is peppered with polite forms of address: 'sir', 'madam', and so on.

The only person not to use such formality within every utterance is Othello. Can you suggest any reasons for that?

Collect together all such examples and divide them between you. Now think of a setting nothing to do with *Othello* and create an improvisation in which you can only use your chosen terms of address.

2 Foreboding (in pairs)

Read through the script opposite. There is a general sense of foreboding. Devise a diagram to show how each of the following contribute to the sense of foreboding:

- sheets
- the dismissal of Emilia
- Barbary's story
- the willow song
- Desdemona's complete obedience.

In each case find a quotation from the script. Explain the implications of each device. Discuss what the dramatic effect might be of this part of the play.

3 Tell the story

What happened to Barbary? Lines 25–9 show there's a story to be told! Write either a tragi-romantic story, a ballad or a short play which narrates the tragic tale of 'Barbary, a woman wronged'. You could experiment with a few ideas first by improvising in a small group.

---

incontinent straight away
approve value

willow willow trees were traditionally symbolic of forsaken lovers

ACT 4   SCENE 3
Cyprus   A room in the castle

Enter OTHELLO, LODOVICO, DESDEMONA,
EMILIA *and* ATTENDANTS

LODOVICO I do beseech you, sir, trouble yourself no further.
OTHELLO O, pardon me; 'twill do me good to walk.
LODOVICO Madam, good night. I humbly thank your ladyship.
DESDEMONA Your honour is most welcome.
OTHELLO Will you walk, sir? O, Desdemona.   5
DESDEMONA My lord?
OTHELLO Get you to bed on th'instant. I will be returned forthwith.
    Dismiss your attendant there. Look't be done.
DESDEMONA I will, my lord.
                Exeunt [Othello, Lodovico and Attendants]
EMILIA How goes it now? He looks gentler than he did.   10
DESDEMONA He says he will return incontinent;
    He hath commanded me to go to bed
    And bade me to dismiss you.
EMILIA   Dismiss me?
DESDEMONA It was his bidding; therefore, good Emilia,
    Give me my nightly wearing, and adieu.   15
    We must not now displease him.
EMILIA I would you had never seen him.
DESDEMONA So would not I: my love doth so approve him
    That even his stubbornness, his checks, his frowns –
    Prithee, unpin me – have grace and favour in them.   20
EMILIA I have laid those sheets you bade me on the bed.
DESDEMONA All's one. Good faith, how foolish are our minds!
    If I do die before thee, prithee shroud me
    In one of those same sheets.
EMILIA   Come, come, you talk.
DESDEMONA My mother had a maid called Barbary: 25
    She was in love, and he she loved proved mad
    And did forsake her. She had a song of willow;
    An old thing 'twas but it expressed her fortune,
    And she died singing it. That song tonight
    Will not go from my mind. I have much to do   30
    But to go hang my head all at one side

HAS A VAGUE FEELING THAT SOMETHING AWFUL WILL HAPPEN

177

Desdemona sings a sad song from her childhood as she prepares for bed.
She and Emilia discuss their differing attitudes to marriage and fidelity.

1 'A proper man' (in pairs)

Desdemona refers to Lodovico as being 'a proper man' (a good-looking man) and someone who 'speaks well'. Emilia agrees. Spend about five minutes discussing why Desdemona says this. What is in her mind?

2 Sing willow (in groups of eight to ten)

Divide up the words of the Willow Song, lines 38–54 (excluding any inserted dialogue) between you. Memorise your line(s) on your own for a few minutes and make sure you know the correct order.

Next, explore ways of presenting the song so as to create a moving dramatic effect. Try whispering or wailing the words. You could experiment with making soft background noises, imitating the sound of wind through branches, or playing with ways of repeating the refrain. Dim the lights if that is possible. Think about how you move as a group, too. Aim at producing a complete theatrical experience, one that is both physical and emotional, expressing Desdemona's mood. And all done within your drama studio or classroom!

3 The Willow Song

One Jacobean edition of the play (published in 1622) omits the song altogether. Perhaps the boy actor who played Desdemona at that time couldn't sing. From your viewing of either a live or videoed performance of the play what was your reaction to the song? What effect did it have on you? Do you think a performance would gain or lose if the song were omitted? Compare your feelings with other students.

---

dispatch hurry up
lay by these put these (clothes) away
hie thee go away

moe more
bode foretell
in conscience honestly

　　　And sing it like poor Barbary – prithee, dispatch.

EMILIA Shall I go fetch your nightgown?

DESDEMONA 　　　　　　　　　　　No, unpin me here.
　　　This Lodovico is a proper man.

EMILIA A very handsome man.

DESDEMONA 　　　　　　　He speaks well. *[not like Othello.]*　　35

EMILIA I know a lady in Venice would have walked barefoot to Palestine
　　for a touch of his nether lip.

DESDEMONA [*Sings*]

　　　The poor soul sat sighing by a sycamore tree,
　　　　Sing all a green willow;
　　　Her hand on her bosom, her head on her knee,　　40
　　　　Sing willow, willow, willow;
　　　The fresh streams ran by her and murmured her moans;
　　　　Sing willow, willow, willow.
　　　Her salt tears fell from her and softened the stones –

Lay by these.　　45
　　　　Sing willow, willow, willow –

Prithee, hie thee; he'll come anon.
　　　Sing all a green willow must be my garland.
　　　Let nobody blame him; his scorn I approve –

Nay that's not next. Hark, who is't that knocks?　　50

EMILIA It's the wind.

DESDEMONA [*Sings*]
　　　I called my love false love, but what said he then?
　　　　Sing willow, willow, willow;
　　　If I court moe women, you'll couch with moe men –

So get thee gone; good night. Mine eyes do itch –　　55
Does that bode weeping?

EMILIA 　　　　　　　　'Tis neither here nor there.

DESDEMONA I have heard it said so. O, these men, these men!
　　Dost thou in conscience think – tell me, Emilia –
　　That there be women do abuse their husbands
　　In such gross kind?

EMILIA 　　　　　　　There be some such, no question.　　60

DESDEMONA Wouldst thou do such a deed for all the world?

EMILIA Why, would not you?

DESDEMONA 　　　　　　No, by this heavenly light.

EMILIA Nor I neither by this heavenly light;
　　I might do't as well i'th'dark.

Emilia says she would commit adultery if it gained her husband the world.
Desdemona can't believe this. Emilia argues that husbands are to blame.

1 Emilia and Desdemona (in pairs)

Compare the two women's views of men and marriage. Would you
agree that one is a romanticised view, whilst the other is much more
practical? Discuss what each woman says in detail. What difference
does their respective social position make to their separate views?

Now, in their own 'voices', role-play Emilia and Desdemona
justifying their views, making reference to their respective social
positions, their own experience of men and married life and their
hopes for the future.

2 Emilia's feminism (in groups of three)

Read lines 82–99 through together. Imagine Emilia is appearing on a
platform as a speaker supporting women's rights. Split the speech up
as you think fit, supplying lines for Emilia's rousing speech on
feminism. Use some lines for questions and answers from the
audience, either supporters or hecklers. Present your version to the
rest of the class.

joint-ring a cheap ring
measures of lawn lengths of fabric
exhibition amount of money
Ud's God's
venture purgatory risk being
condemned to the torture of
Purgatory

to th'advantage in addition
store populate
treasures sexual favours
in despite out of spite
galls the guts to get revenge

DESDEMONA Wouldst thou do such a deed for all the world?   65
EMILIA The world's a huge thing; it is a great price
    For a small vice.
DESDEMONA   In troth, I think thou wouldst not.
EMILIA In troth, I think I should, and undo't when I had done it.
    Marry, I would not do such a thing for a joint-ring, nor for
    measures of lawn, nor for gowns, petticoats, nor caps, nor any   70
    petty exhibition. But for all the whole world! Ud's pity,
    who would not make her husband a cuckold, to make him a
    monarch? I should venture purgatory for't.
DESDEMONA Beshrew me, if I would do such a wrong for the whole
    world.   75
EMILIA Why, the wrong is but a wrong i'th'world; and having the world
    for your labour, 'tis a wrong in your own world, and you might
    quickly make it right.
DESDEMONA I do not think there is any such woman.
EMILIA Yes, a dozen; and as many to th'advantage as would store   80
    the world they played for.
        But I do think it is their husbands' faults
        If wives do fall. Say that they slack their duties
        And pour our treasures into foreign laps,
        Or else break out in peevish jealousies,   85
        Throwing restraint upon us; or say they strike us,
        Or scant our former having in despite –
        Why, we have galls, and though we have some grace,
        Yet have we some revenge. Let husbands know
        Their wives have sense like them: they see, and smell,   90
        And have their palates both for sweet and sour
        As husbands have. What is it that they do
        When they change us for others? Is it sport?
        I think it is. And doth affection breed it?
        I think it doth. Is't frailty that thus errs?   95
        It is so too. And have not we affections,
        Desires for sport, and frailty, as men have?
        Then let them use us well; else let them know
        The ills we do, their ills instruct us so.
DESDEMONA Good night, good night. God me such uses send,   100
    Not to pick bad from bad, but by bad mend!
                                    Exeunt

Looking back at Act 4

1 Intercut two scenes (in groups of three)

Desdemona kneels to Iago to enlist his help in 4.2.150. Not only is this heavy with very obvious irony, but also parallels the scene where Othello kneels before Iago to swear vengeance (3.3.451).

Turn to these two references and read the relevant sections of surrounding script. Experiment to find a way of intercutting (interweaving) the two episodes where husband and wife both kneel unwittingly before their tormentor.

2 Abuse of Desdemona (in groups of about ten)

This activity is both an exploration of Desdemona's experience and social position, and of Othello's use of increasingly crude and abusive language in Act 4. The following lines are all spoken by Othello directly to Desdemona's face:

'thou art false as hell'
'look grim as hell'
'O, thou weed'
'was this fair paper . . ./Made to write "whore" upon?'
'O, thou public commoner!'
'Impudent strumpet!'
'Are not you a strumpet?'
'What, not a whore?'
'I took you for that cunning whore of Venice'
'We have done our course'.

Take and learn one of the above lines each. Move around the room and every time you encounter another student shout, hiss or sneer your line in their face.

Next, stand in a long line, all facing one way. Go swiftly down the row, spinning round one by one so that you are facing the next person and snap out your lines. Then try standing in a tight circle with one student kneeling in the middle. Hurl your lines of abuse at him/her.

Try different ways of presenting the lines – perhaps you could form a 'speaking tableau' to suggest the roles and relationship of Othello and Desdemona. Experiment!

3 An *Othello* glossary

During the course of the play, Iago completely redefines the word 'honest'. Othello redefines and distorts the meaning of 'justice'. These are not the only words which change their meaning or effect through the play.

Compile an *Othello* glossary, defining words in terms of the way they come to be used in the course of the play. Here is a list of suggested entries you might have in your glossary:

- justice
- honesty
- whore
- savage
- civility

(others might include 'noble', 'valiant', 'ocular proof').

For each give one or two examples of their usage in the script. You might like to employ a suitably ironic tone in your writing for this activity!

Laurence Olivier as Othello and Maggie Smith as Desdemona, National Theatre production (1964).

Iago positions Roderigo for the murder. He hopes both Cassio and Roderigo will die. Roderigo fails to kill Cassio, who wounds him instead. Iago leaps out of hiding, strikes Cassio and runs off.

1 Intrigue again

Act 5 opens in a very similar way to Act 1, with Iago and Roderigo plotting villainy in the streets, late at night. What other similarities are there with that opening scene – and what key differences?

2 Iago reveals his thoughts (in pairs)

Read through Iago's aside, lines 11–22. The early nineteenth-century poet and writer, Samuel Taylor Coleridge, was intrigued by the character of Iago, whose activities he described as arising out of 'motiveless malignity'. Yet Iago himself has already given us several reasons for his vendetta against Othello and Cassio, and in this aside he adds to the list of possible reasons. Discuss first what you think is meant by Iago's comment 'He hath a daily beauty in his life that makes me ugly' (lines 19–20). Then talk together about Iago's motivation (or lack of it) to do harm to others and whether you think that Coleridge was right in his assessment.

3 Slow motion (in groups of four)

Show the action in slow motion from line 22, 'But soft, I hear him coming' to Othello's entrance at line 27.

bulk projecting wall	**live Roderigo** if Roderigo lives
straight immediately	**bobbed** conned, tricked
quat spot or boil	**unfold** expose

Act 5 Scene 1
Cyprus A street at night

Enter IAGO *and* RODERIGO

IAGO Here, stand behind this bulk; straight will he come.
  Wear thy good rapier bare, and put it home.
  Quick, quick, fear nothing; I'll be at thy elbow.
  It makes us or it mars us; think on that,
  And fix most firm thy resolution.   5
RODERIGO Be near at hand; I may miscarry in't.
IAGO Here, at thy hand; be bold, and take thy stand.
            [*He retires.*]
RODERIGO I have no great devotion to the deed,
  And yet he hath given me satisfying reasons.
  'Tis but a man gone. Forth my sword! He dies!   10
IAGO [*Aside*] I have rubbed this young quat almost to the sense,
  And he grows angry. Now, whether he kill Cassio,
  Or Cassio him, or each do kill the other,
  Every way makes my gain. Live Roderigo,
  He calls me to a restitution large   15
  Of gold and jewels that I bobbed from him
  As gifts to Desdemona.
  It must not be. If Cassio do remain,
  He hath a daily beauty in his life
  That makes me ugly; and besides, the Moor   20
  May unfold me to him – there stand I in much peril.
  No, he must die. But soft, I hear him coming.

Enter CASSIO.

RODERIGO I know his gait; 'tis he. Villain, thou diest!
          [*He lunges at Cassio.*]
CASSIO That thrust had been mine enemy indeed
  But that my coat is better than thou think'st.   25
  I will make proof of thine.
         [*He wounds Roderigo.*]
RODERIGO   O, I am slain!
       [*Iago wounds Cassio in the leg and exit*]
CASSIO I am maimed forever. Help, ho! Murder, murder!

Enter OTHELLO.

185

Othello hears the scuffles and, satisfied Cassio is dead, goes off to kill Desdemona. Lodovico and Gratiano cautiously investigate the cries of the two wounded men. Iago arrives to help.

1 Who's doing what when? (in pairs)

There has been much action in the last fifty-five lines. As you can imagine, on stage it is both quick-moving and exciting.

Here is one person's idea for staging it on the stage of Shakespeare's Globe. The drawing shows different characters at different moments and the events are numbered in the order in which they happen in the script.

Decide who each person is in the drawing and work out which moment in the script is being represented in each case. Find a suitable quotation for each one (five in all).

minion darling (used contemptuously about Desdemona)
hies is coming fast
blotted wiped out

watch night patrol
passage passers-by
heavy dark
spoiled wounded

OTHELLO [*Aside*] The voice of Cassio: Iago keeps his word.
RODERIGO O villain that I am!
OTHELLO [*Aside*]   It is even so.
CASSIO O help, ho! Light! A surgeon!   30
OTHELLO [*Aside*] 'Tis he. O brave Iago, honest and just,
      That hast such noble sense of thy friend's wrong!
      Thou teachest me. Minion, your dear lies dead,
      And your unblest fate hies. Strumpet, I come!
      Forth of my heart those charms, thine eyes, are blotted;   35
      Thy bed, lust-stained, shall with lust's blood be spotted.
                                                    Exit Othello

                Enter LODOVICO *and* GRATIANO.

CASSIO What, ho! No watch? No passage? Murder, murder!
GRATIANO 'Tis some mischance; the cry is very direful.
CASSIO O, help!
LODOVICO Hark!   40
RODERIGO O, wretched villain!
LODOVICO Two or three groan. It is a heavy night.
      These may be counterfeits: let's think't unsafe
      To come in to the cry without more help.
RODERIGO Nobody come? Then I shall bleed to death.   45
LODOVICO Hark!

                Enter Iago, with a light.

GRATIANO Here's one comes in his shirt, with light and weapons.
IAGO Who's there? Whose noise is this that cries on murder?
LODOVICO We do not know.
IAGO   Did you not hear a cry?
CASSIO Here, here; for heaven's sake, help me!
IAGO   What's the matter?   50
GRATIANO This is Othello's ancient, as I take it.
LODOVICO The same indeed, a very valiant fellow.
IAGO What are you here that cry so grievously?
CASSIO Iago? O, I am spoiled, undone by villains!
      Give me some help.   55

In pretending to investigate what has happened, Iago secretly stabs the wounded Roderigo. Cassio is discovered to have a severe leg wound. Bianca arrives to see what's happened and Iago insults her.

1 Tableaux (in groups of six)

Prepare and present a series of four tableaux (or 'still photographs') from key moments of the scene so far:

'What villains have done this?' (line 56)

'O damned Iago' (line 62)

'Are you of good or evil?' (line 65)

'. . . Cassio, may you suspect

Who they should be that have thus mangled you?' (lines 78–9).

Each person takes on a role. Decide as a group where each character would be positioned, what emotion might be registered on their face and so on.

Share your tableaux with the other groups. Can they guess the characters in each? Discuss different interpretations that occur.

2 How fast? (in groups of four or five)

The script is full of short sentences. To catch the mood and the speed of the action, try these ways of reading lines 56–84:

a read around the group, each person exclaiming a single sentence only before handing on

b repeat the exercise, but this time exclaim only one word – the one you think most important – in each sentence

c repeat both exercises, but as quickly as possible.

Afterwards, talk together about the speed at which you think the lines should be spoken.

Marry mild swearing (literally 'by the Virgin Mary')

IAGO O me, lieutenant! What villains have done this?
CASSIO I think that one of them is hereabout
       And cannot make away.
IAGO   O, treacherous villains!
       [*To Lodovico and Gratiano*] What are you there? Come in,
         and give some help.
RODERIGO O, help me here!   60
CASSIO That's one of them.
IAGO   O murderous slave! O villain!
       [*He stabs Roderigo.*]
RODERIGO O damned Iago! O inhuman dog!
       [*He faints.*]
IAGO Kill men i'th'dark? Where be these bloody thieves?
       How silent is this town! Ho, murder, murder!
        [*Lodovico and Gratiano come forward.*]
       What may you be? Are you of good or evil?   65
LODOVICO As you shall prove us, praise us.
IAGO Signior Lodovico?
LODOVICO He, sir.
IAGO I cry you mercy. Here's Cassio hurt by villains.
GRATIANO Cassio?   70
IAGO How is't, brother?
CASSIO My leg is cut in two.
IAGO   Marry, heaven forbid!
       Light, gentlemen. I'll bind it with my shirt.

         Enter BIANCA.

BIANCA What is the matter, ho? Who is't that cried?
IAGO Who is't that cried?   75
BIANCA O, my dear Cassio, my sweet Cassio!
       O, Cassio, Cassio, Cassio!
IAGO O notable strumpet! Cassio, may you suspect
       Who they should be that have thus mangled you?
CASSIO No.   80
GRATIANO I am sorry to find you thus; I have been to seek you.

Iago accuses Bianca of involvement in the affray. He pretends to be surprised at identifying Roderigo as Cassio's attacker. He shows great concern for Cassio, and has him carried off to receive treatment.

1 What if . . .? (in groups of five or six)

Iago seems to have avoided personal disaster very narrowly, by a combination of mere chance and his own skill. However, if Lodovico and Gratiano had been more courageous and had immediately and properly investigated the screams from the street (line 37), the whole scene might have unfolded in a very different way. Improvise what *might* have happened from the point of Lodovico and Gratiano's entrance.

2 Bianca's statement

Iago is so confidently in his stride he doesn't hesitate to cast doubt on Bianca, calling her 'this trash'. He insinuates (lines 105–10) that she might be an accessory to the murder. Over the page you will find that Bianca becomes an easy target for Emilia, too, who calls her a 'strumpet' (whilst Cassio is a 'poor victim'!).

Imagine you are Bianca and write a short statement defending yourself against Iago's charge. Practise reading it in role, and share it with the rest of the class.

---

trash rubbish (referring to Bianca)
a chair probably a sedan chair to
  carry off Cassio

IAGO Lend me a garter: so. O for a chair
    To bear him easily hence!
BIANCA   Alas, he faints!
    O, Cassio, Cassio, Cassio!
IAGO Gentlemen all, I do suspect this trash   85
    To be a party in this injury.
    Patience awhile, good Cassio. Come, come,
    Lend me a light. Know we this face or no?
    Alas, my friend and my dear countryman!
    Roderigo? No – yes, sure – O, heaven, Roderigo!   90
GRATIANO What, of Venice?
IAGO Even he, sir; did you know him?
GRATIANO   Know him? Ay.
IAGO Signior Gratiano! I cry your gentle pardon.
    These bloody accidents must excuse my manners
    That so neglected you.
GRATIANO   I am glad to see you.   95
IAGO How do you, Cassio? O, a chair, a chair!
GRATIANO Roderigo?
IAGO He, he, 'tis he.

           [Enter ATTENDANTS *with a chair.]*
          O, that's well said, the chair!
    Some good men bear him carefully from hence.
    I'll fetch the general's surgeon. *[To Bianca]* For you,
        mistress,   100
    Save you your labour. – He that lies slain here, Cassio,
    Was my dear friend. What malice was between you?
CASSIO None in the world, nor do I know the man.
IAGO *[To Bianca]* What, look you pale? – O, bear him out o'th'air.
         [Cassio is carried off; Roderigo's body is removed]

*Iago accuses Bianca of looking guilty. He explains what's happened to
Emilia who verbally abuses Bianca. Iago sends Emilia to Othello
with the news.*

1 Guilty looks (in pairs)

Can you tell if a person is guilty by the way she looks (lines 109–10)?
Talk together about how Bianca probably looks at this moment.

2 Fast forward (in groups of eight to ten)

For this activity you are going to need to work in a large, clear space
because you'll be rushing around! So either clear a space in the
classroom or use the drama studio or hall.

Think of old silent movies when the action gets ridiculously
fast-moving, and is usually accompanied by breathlessly rapid music.
Or think what happens when you hold down the 'fast forward' control
on a video player and the action becomes comically frenetic. Try
staging Act 5, Scene 1 as if it's being played like that. You will find the
need for speed adds to your understanding of the sequence of events.
If you do it properly you should be completely out of breath at the
end!

To make it more fun, find some suitable musical accompaniment:
'The Flight of the Bumble-Bee' or old silent movie chase music . . .

3 Afterwards . . .

While you are still catching your breath, sit in a circle and go
immediately into a reading of the next scene. That way you will gain
an appreciation of the dramatic change in tone and pace between
Scenes 1 and 2.

---

gastness terrified look
dressed have wounds treated
fordoes me quite ruins me
  completely

Stay you, good gentlemen. Look you pale, mistress? 105
Do you perceive the gastness of her eye?
[*To Bianca*] Nay, if you stare, we shall hear more anon.
Behold her well; I pray you, look upon her.
Do you see, gentlemen? Nay, guiltiness
Will speak, though tongues were out of use. 110

Enter EMILIA.

EMILIA 'Las, what's the matter? What's the matter, husband?
IAGO Cassio hath here been set on in the dark
    By Roderigo and fellows that are 'scaped.
    He's almost slain and Roderigo dead.
EMILIA Alas, good gentleman! Alas, good Cassio! 115
IAGO This is the fruits of whoring. Prithee, Emilia,
    Go know of Cassio where he supped tonight.
    [*To Bianca*] What, do you shake at that?
BIANCA He supped at my house, but I therefore shake not.
IAGO O, did he so? I charge you go with me. 120
EMILIA O, fie upon thee, strumpet!
BIANCA I am no strumpet, but of life as honest
    As you that thus abuse me.
EMILIA   As I? Foh! Fie upon thee!
IAGO Kind gentlemen, let's go see poor Cassio dressed.
    Come, mistress, you must tell's another tale. 125
    Emilia, run you to the citadel
    And tell my lord and lady what hath happed.
    Will you go on afore? [*Aside*] This is the night
    That either makes me, or fordoes me quite.
                            Exeunt

Othello reasons why Desdemona must die and that the dead cannot be restored to life. He kisses her and nearly abandons his intent to kill her, but resolves that she must die.

1 Othello's 'cause' (in groups of three or four)

Othello repeats the word 'cause' three times in the opening three lines of the new scene. For the Elizabethans, 'cause' could carry several meanings:

- an action which prompts a reaction (Desdemona's infidelity)
- a morally justifiable end one is pursuing, 'all in a good cause' (Othello wishing to protect 'more men' and restore moral order)
- a legal usage meaning an accusation brought against someone in court (Othello sees himself as an agent of impartial justice).

Take the phrase 'It is the cause' and illustrate these three meanings in a way which relates to Othello's situation and state of mind at this point in the play. Use whatever dramatic method of presentation which seems appropriate to you.

2 Images: avoiding reality? (in groups of four to six)

Lines 1–22 are rich in images. One writer has suggested that Othello cannot bring himself to face the reality of his own role, the living woman before him and his intended act, so he finds symbols for each in an attempt to idealise his situation. Talk together about how the following images are used:

a carved alabaster effigy on a tomb
light
the figure of Justice (usually depicted with sword and scales)
a rose.

Divide the lines of the speech between the members of your group. Either learn your 'chunk' of text or write it down on card. Find ways of presenting the speech so that all group members are actively involved, and the verbal imagery is made clear.

---

flaming minister burning torch
Promethean heat in Greek
  mythology Prometheus stole fire

from the gods and used it to give
life to mortals
relume light again

ACT 5   SCENE 2
Cyprus   Desdemona's bedchamber

Enter OTHELLO, *with a light, and* DESDEMONA *in bed*

OTHELLO It is the cause, it is the cause, my soul:
  Let me not name it to you, you chaste stars.
  It is the cause. Yet I'll not shed her blood,
  Nor scar that whiter skin of hers than snow
  And smooth as monumental alabaster –   5
  Yet she must die, else she'll betray more men.
  Put out the light, and then put out the light:
  If I quench thee, thou flaming minister,
  I can again thy former light restore,
  Should I repent me; but once put out thy light,   10
  Thou cunning'st pattern of excelling nature,
  I know not where is that Promethean heat
  That can thy light relume. When I have plucked thy rose,
  I cannot give it vital growth again;
  It needs must wither. I'll smell it on the tree.   15
                    He kisses her.
  O balmy breath, that dost almost persuade
  Justice to break her sword! One more, one more!
  Be thus when thou art dead, and I will kill thee
  And love thee after. One more, and this the last.
  So sweet was ne'er so fatal. I must weep.   20
  But they are cruel tears: this sorrow's heavenly –
  It strikes where it doth love. She wakes.

[Handwritten annotations: "Justice", "She must die before she betrays anyone else", "very final"]

195

Desdemona wakes. Othello orders her to confess her sins before her death. Desdemona, fearful, replies her sin is in loving him.

1 Read through – and actions (in pairs)

Desdemona apparently begins this scene lying asleep in her bed. What do you think might be her subsequent movements? Take the roles of Othello and Desdemona and read lines 1–85 to each other, suggesting movement and action at appropriate points.

solicit pray for forgiveness
straight at once

forfend forbid
portents bad signs for the future

DESDEMONA Who's there? Othello?
OTHELLO   Ay, Desdemona.
DESDEMONA Will you come to bed, my lord?
OTHELLO Have you prayed tonight, Desdemon?
DESDEMONA   Ay, my lord.   25
OTHELLO If you bethink yourself of any crime
　　　　Unreconciled as yet to heaven and grace,
　　　　Solicit for it straight.
DESDEMONA Alack, my lord, what may you mean by that?
OTHELLO Well, do it, and be brief: I will walk by: 30
　　　　I would not kill thy unpreparèd spirit;
　　　　No – heaven forfend! – I would not kill thy soul.
DESDEMONA Talk you of killing?
OTHELLO   Ay, I do.
DESDEMONA   Then heaven
　　　　Have mercy on me!
OTHELLO   Amen, with all my heart!
DESDEMONA If you say so, I hope you will not kill me.   35
OTHELLO Hum!
DESDEMONA And yet I fear you, for you're fatal then
　　　　When your eyes roll so. Why I should fear I know not,
　　　　Since guiltiness I know not, but yet I feel I fear.
OTHELLO Think on thy sins.
DESDEMONA   They are loves I bear to you.   40
OTHELLO Ay, and for that thou diest.
DESDEMONA That death's unnatural that kills for loving.
　　　　Alas, why gnaw you so your nether lip?
　　　　Some bloody passion shakes your very frame:
　　　　These are portents; but yet I hope, I hope   45
　　　　They do not point on me.

Othello accuses Desdemona of giving her handkerchief to Cassio. She denies this, yet Othello is convinced he has enough proof. He tells her that Cassio has confessed to sexual relations with Desdemona, but now is dead.

1 Justice enacted? (in groups of three)

There is much legal language in this bedroom scene, almost as if it were some kind of courtroom in session, with Othello taking on the roles of both judge and executioner. Pick out any examples of legal-sounding language you can find. Identify what constitutes the case for the prosecution, the case for the defence and what is presented as evidence. How does Othello's 'legal procedure' differ from what you know to be conventional practice?

Enact a version of this section of the scene as if it is taking place in a court of law. Play with the script as much as you like, but retain fragments of the original language. Try playing it in different styles and tones (for example, as a parody of a television courtroom drama).

2 Two statues (in pairs)

Create a statue or sculpture entitled 'The Sacrifice', followed by one called 'A Murder'. Share your tableaux with the rest of the class, and discuss what essential differences you perceive there to be between the two concepts.

Relate your explorations of the two terms to Othello's words at line 65.

---

perjury untruthfulness, lying on oath
presently at once
article an item in a list of accusations (a legal term)

conception suspicion
groan withal am pained by, give birth to

OTHELLO   Peace, and be still!

DESDEMONA I will so. What's the matter?

OTHELLO That handkerchief which I so loved and gave thee,
        Thou gav'st to Cassio.

DESDEMONA   No, by my life and soul!
        Send for the man and ask him.

OTHELLO   Sweet soul, take heed.   50
        Take heed of perjury: thou art on thy death-bed.

DESDEMONA Ay, but not yet to die.

OTHELLO   Yes, presently.
        Therefore confess thee freely of thy sin;
        For to deny each article with oath
        Cannot remove nor choke the strong conception   55
        That I do groan withal. Thou art to die.

DESDEMONA Then Lord have mercy on me!

OTHELLO   I say, Amen.

DESDEMONA And have you mercy too! I never did
        Offend you in my life; never loved Cassio
        But with such general warranty of heaven   60
        As I might love. I never gave him token.

OTHELLO By heaven, I saw my handkerchief in's hand.
        O perjured woman! Thou dost stone my heart,
        And mak'st me call what I intend to do
        A murder, which I thought a sacrifice.   65
        I saw the handkerchief.

DESDEMONA   He found it then;
        I never gave it him. Send for him hither;
        Let him confess a truth.

OTHELLO   He hath confessed.

DESDEMONA What, my lord?

OTHELLO That he hath used thee.

DESDEMONA   How? Unlawfully?   70

OTHELLO Ay.

DESDEMONA He will not say so.

OTHELLO   No, his mouth is stopped:
        Honest Iago hath tane order for't.

DESDEMONA O, my fear interprets! What, is he dead?

OTHELLO Had all his hairs been lives, my great revenge   75
        Had stomach for them all.

In spite of her pleas, Othello suffocates Desdemona. He is disturbed by Emilia calling from outside the door.

---

1 Action – avoiding melodrama (in groups of three or four)

Act line 78 ('Out strumpet!') to line 106 ('What's the matter . . .?'). Make decisions about the pace, timing of stage directions, positioning and delivery of words to suit the dramatic effect you wish to achieve. How do you avoid it becoming melodramatic, and therefore bordering on the ridiculous?

Share your version with one other group, then discuss any differences of interpretation. Can you combine your ideas to put together another, improved 'production'?

2 'Cruel' but 'merciful' (in pairs)

Can you agree with Othello's estimation of himself as:

'I that am cruel am yet merciful'?

Spend about five minutes discussing what reasons Othello has to make such a claim about himself.

3 Shakespeare's source

In the story by Cinthio from which Shakespeare took his basic idea for *Othello*, Desdemona is killed by the Ensign who hides in Desdemona's closet and clubs her to death with a stocking filled with sand. In order to make it look like an accident, the counterpart of Othello rigs up the four poster bed so that it collapses on her body.

Assess the changes Shakespeare has made to this part of the story in terms of artistic appropriateness and the practicalities of the theatre.

---

undone ruined
being done . . . pause now I've started, I can't stop

yawn tear apart (in an earthquake)

DESDEMONA Alas, he is betrayed, and I undone.
OTHELLO Out, strumpet! Weep'st thou for him to my face?
DESDEMONA O banish me, my lord, but kill me not!
OTHELLO Down, strumpet!   80
DESDEMONA Kill me tomorrow; let me live tonight!
OTHELLO Nay, if you strive –
DESDEMONA But half an hour!
OTHELLO   Being done, there is no pause.
DESDEMONA But while I say one prayer!
OTHELLO   It is too late.
DESDEMONA O, Lord, Lord, Lord!   85
                    He smothers her.
EMILIA (*Within*) My lord, my lord! What, ho! My lord, my lord!
OTHELLO What noise is this? Not dead? Not yet quite dead?
    I that am cruel am yet merciful;
    I would not have thee linger in thy pain.
    So, so.
EMILIA (*Within*) What, ho! My lord, my lord!
OTHELLO   Who's there?   90
EMILIA [*Within*] O, good my lord, I would speak a word with you.
OTHELLO Yes – 'tis Emilia – by and by. – She's dead.
    'Tis like she comes to speak of Cassio's death:
    The noise was high. Ha! No more moving?
    Still as the grave. Shall she come in? Were't good?   95
    I think she stirs again. No. What's best to do?
    If she come in, she'll sure speak to my wife –
    My wife, my wife! What wife? I have no wife.
    O insupportable! O heavy hour!
    Methinks it should be now a huge eclipse   100
    Of sun and moon, and that th'affrighted globe
    Should yawn at alteration.
EMILIA [*Within*]   I do beseech you
    That I may speak with you. O, good my lord!
OTHELLO I had forgot thee. O, come in, Emilia.
    Soft, by and by. Let me the curtains draw.   105
    Where art thou?
                    [*He unlocks the door.*]
                    What's the matter with thee now?

Emilia tells that Roderigo is dead but Cassio lives. Desdemona revives briefly, only to protect her husband in her dying breath. Othello confesses to Emilia and attempts to explain.

---

1 Desdemona (in groups of three or four)

Even in her dying breath, Desdemona supports her husband. She even tells a lie on her death-bed to protect him from a murder charge. Do you admire her for her faithfulness, or find her action rather hard to swallow? Do you see her as a dramatic function, a sharp contrast to Othello, rather than as a 'real' person?

Discuss your attitudes to the way Desdemona has been portrayed throughout Act 5. Focus your discussion on:

- how late twentieth-century readers might react to Desdemona;
- how the reader's gender and culture also affects the way s/he sees Desdemona;
- how Desdemona reflects early seventeenth-century attitudes to women and marriage;
- how Desdemona embodies or relates to the play's dramatic themes and concerns.

2 Contrasts (in pairs)

Opposite are a number of sharp contrasts in language:

angel	v	devil
false	v	true
water	v	fire
heaven	v	hell
sweet	v	harsh.

Locate each pair in the page of script opposite. Share them between you and explore ways of presenting them through movement or tableaux.

Talk together about the significance of each pair of contrasts in their dramatic context.

---

error of the moon the moon straying off course (the influence of the moon was said to cause madness)

was wont used to do

Enter EMILIA.

EMILIA O, my good lord, yonder's foul murders done.

OTHELLO What? Now?

EMILIA But now, my lord.

OTHELLO It is the very error of the moon: 110
          She comes more nearer earth than she was wont
          And makes men mad.

EMILIA Cassio, my lord, hath killed a young Venetian
          Called Roderigo.

OTHELLO   Roderigo killed?
          And Cassio killed?

EMILIA   No, Cassio is not killed.   115

OTHELLO Not Cassio killed! Then murder's out of tune,
          And sweet revenge grows harsh.

DESDEMONA O, falsely, falsely murdered!

EMILIA   O Lord! What cry is that?

OTHELLO That? What?

EMILIA Out and alas, that was my lady's voice!   120
              [*She draws the bed-curtains.*]
          Help, help, ho, help! O, lady, speak again!
          Sweet Desdemona, O sweet mistress, speak!

DESDEMONA A guiltless death I die.

EMILIA O, who hath done this deed?

DESDEMONA Nobody; I myself. Farewell.   125
          Commend me to my kind lord. O farewell!   *She dies*

OTHELLO Why, how should she be murdered?

EMILIA   Alas, who knows?

OTHELLO You heard her say herself it was not I.

EMILIA She said so; I must needs report the truth.

OTHELLO She's like a liar gone to burning hell: 130
          'Twas I that killed her.

EMILIA   O, the more angel she,
          And you the blacker devil!

OTHELLO She turned to folly, and she was a whore.

EMILIA Thou dost belie her, and thou art a devil.

OTHELLO She was false as water.

EMILIA   Thou art rash as fire to say   135
          That she was false. O, she was heavenly true!

Othello reveals that Iago gave him the details of Desdemona's infidelity. Emilia increasingly questions Iago's part in Othello's story and curses them both. She is unmoved by Othello's threats and calls for help.

1 Emilia (in groups of six to eight)

As you read the page of script, pay particular attention to the role and character of Emilia. Select a word, phrase or line of hers which strikes you as being interesting or memorable. Learn your chosen word(s).

Present your 'collective memory' of Emilia by putting together a group presentation of all your chosen fragments of script. It doesn't matter if some of you have chosen the same words. Combine the words with stylised movement, or some other action.

2 'Husband' (in pairs)

As a class, collect together a pile of various everyday objects (for example, umbrella, milk bottle, briefcase, cardboard box, newspaper). Each pair selects an object. Now put together an improvisation around your object – but the only word you can use is 'husband'!

3 'Honest, honest Iago' (in groups of three)

The ten repetitions of the word 'husband' culminate in Othello's exclamation: 'My friend, thy husband, honest, honest Iago'.

Produce a series of 'sculptures' (using yourselves as the 'raw material') which are based on any ideas which arise from your interpretation of line 153 within its context in the play.

4 'Ha!'

Spend about five minutes writing what you think Othello means by his exclamation 'Ha!' at line 157. Compare your notes with others and discuss what led to your interpretation.

---

else if you don't believe it
extremity final punishment (legal term)
chrysolite a semi-precious stone

made mocks with mocked
peace . . . best you'd better keep quiet

OTHELLO Cassio did top her: ask thy husband else.
  O, I were damned beneath all depth in hell
  But that I did proceed upon just grounds
  To this extremity. Thy husband knew it all.   140
EMILIA My husband?
OTHELLO   Thy husband.
EMILIA   That she was false to wedlock?
OTHELLO Ay, with Cassio. Nay, had she been true,
  If heaven would make me such another world
  Of one entire and perfect chrysolite,
  I'd not have sold her for it.
EMILIA   My husband?   145
OTHELLO Ay, 'twas he that told me on her first;
  An honest man he is, and hates the slime
  That sticks on filthy deeds.
EMILIA   My husband?
OTHELLO What needs this iterance, woman? I say thy husband.
EMILIA O mistress, villainy hath made mocks with love!   150
  My husband say that she was false?
OTHELLO   He, woman;
  I say thy husband. Dost understand the word?
  My friend, thy husband, honest, honest Iago.
EMILIA If he say so, may his pernicious soul
  Rot half a grain a day! He lies to th'heart.   155
  She was too fond of her most filthy bargain.
OTHELLO Ha!
EMILIA Do thy worst.
  This deed of thine is no more worthy heaven
  Than thou wast worthy her.
OTHELLO   Peace, you were best.   160
EMILIA Thou hast not half that power to do me harm
  As I have to be hurt. O gull! O dolt!
  As ignorant as dirt. Thou hast done a deed –
  I care not for thy sword – I'll make thee known,
  Though I lost twenty lives. Help! help! ho, help!   165
  The Moor hath killed my mistress. Murder, murder!

> *Montano, Gratiano and Iago come to investigate Emilia's cries of murder. She challenges Iago about what he has told Othello about Desdemona. Iago orders her home.*

1 Four photographs (in groups of five or six)

Imagine photographing the action on stage at four key moments from this page of script:

a 'Disprove this villain, if thou be'st a man' (line 171)
b 'O monstrous act!' (line 189)
c 'What, are you mad?' (line 193)
d '. . . thou hast killed the sweetest innocent
     That e'er did lift up eye' (lines 198–9).

Take roles, and for each 'moment' create a still picture which you can hold for at least thirty seconds. Within each, select a key character who can step out of the photograph and outline their personal thoughts or fears at that precise moment.

Present your four moments to the rest of the class as a series of snapshots.

---

charm hold still
forfend forbid

set the murder on caused the
  murder

Enter MONTANO, GRATIANO *and* IAGO.

MONTANO What is the matter? How now, general?

EMILIA O, are you come, Iago? You have done well,
That men must lay their murders on your neck.

GRATIANO What is the matter?   170

EMILIA Disprove this villain, if thou be'st a man.
He says thou told'st him that his wife was false.
I know thou didst not, thou'rt not such a villain.
Speak, for my heart is full.

IAGO I told him what I thought, and told no more   175
Than what he found himself was apt and true.

EMILIA But did you ever tell him she was false?

IAGO I did.

EMILIA You told a lie, an odious damnèd lie:
Upon my soul, a lie, a wicked lie!   180
She false with Cassio? Did you say with Cassio?

IAGO With Cassio, mistress. Go to, charm your tongue.

EMILIA I will not charm my tongue; I am bound to speak:
My mistress here lies murdered in her bed.

ALL O, heavens forfend!   185

EMILIA And your reports have set the murder on.

OTHELLO Nay, stare not, masters; it is true indeed.

GRATIANO 'Tis a strange truth.

MONTANO O monstrous act!

EMILIA   Villainy, villainy, villainy!
I think upon't, I think – I smell't – O villainy!   190
I thought so then; I'll kill myself for grief.
O villainy, villainy!

IAGO What, are you mad? I charge you get you home.

EMILIA Good gentlemen, let me have leave to speak.
'Tis proper I obey him, but not now.   195
Perchance, Iago, I will ne'er go home.

OTHELLO O! O! O!

Othello falls on the bed.

EMILIA   Nay, lay thee down and roar,
For thou hast killed the sweetest innocent
That e'er did lift up eye.

207

Othello confesses the murder to Gratiano, who tells that Brabantio is dead. Emilia reveals that Iago persuaded her to steal Desdemona's handkerchief and give it to him. Iago tries to silence her.

1 Flashback (in groups of four)

Othello claims that Desdemona committed 'the act of shame' many times with Cassio, and that 'Cassio confessed it'. Remind yourself exactly what Cassio 'confessed' to, and in what circumstances. There are three versions of this 'evidence': Iago's, Othello's and Cassio's. Flick back to Act 4.1.72–153. Using mime plus commentary show this episode from the point of view of Cassio, Othello or Iago.

Pick three groups who have chosen different viewpoints and show their 'flashbacks' in succession.

2 Thoughts (in pairs)

At line 221, Iago draws his sword and threatens Emilia. Work out what you think their separate thoughts are at that precise moment. You could begin by freezing on the stage direction, then relaxing in turn to reveal your thoughts.

3 Desdemona's father

Gratiano reports Brabantio's death in lines 203–8. Brabantio must often have thought of Desdemona. Write the letter he sends to her on his death-bed.

---

mortal fatal
shore cut
thread thread of life

reprobance state of damnation
recognisance keepsake
north either north wind, or people of the north

OTHELLO [*Standing up.*]   O, she was foul!
    I scarce did know you, uncle; there lies your niece,   200
    Whose breath indeed these hands have newly stopped.
    I know this act shows horrible and grim –
GRATIANO Poor Desdemon, I am glad thy father's dead:
    Thy match was mortal to him, and pure grief
    Shore his old thread in twain. Did he live now,   205
    This sight would make him do a desperate turn,
    Yea, curse his better angel from his side
    And fall to reprobance.
OTHELLO 'Tis pitiful; but yet Iago knows
    That she with Cassio hath the act of shame   210
    A thousand times committed. Cassio confessed it,
    And she did gratify his amorous works
    With that recognisance and pledge of love
    Which I first gave her. I saw it in his hand:
    It was a handkerchief, an antique token   215
    My father gave my mother.
EMILIA   O God! O heavenly God!
IAGO Zounds, hold your peace!
EMILIA   'Twill out, 'twill out. I peace!
    No, I will speak as liberal as the north;
    Let heaven, and men, and devils, let them all,
    All, all cry shame against me, yet I'll speak.   220
IAGO Be wise and get you home.
EMILIA   I will not.
                    [*Iago draws his sword and threatens Emilia.*]
GRATIANO   Fie,
    Your sword upon a woman!
EMILIA O thou dull Moor, that handkerchief thou speak'st of
    I found by fortune and did give my husband,
    For often, with a solemn earnestness –
    More than indeed belonged to such a trifle –   225
    He begged of me to steal it.
IAGO   Villainous whore!

209

Othello attempts to kill Iago, but is prevented by Montano. Iago stabs
Emilia and then escapes. Emilia dies speaking of Desdemona's purity.
Othello finds another sword and calls to Gratiano.

1 Slow motion (in groups of five or six)

Enact the stage direction at line 233 in slow motion. Decide how you could make the best use of the space you have available, and experiment with different ways of making an intensely dramatic scene.

Turn to the plan of an Elizabethan theatre on page 186 and plot the same action in that space.

2 What do you think?

Take Othello's comment: 'why should honour outlive honesty?' (line 243). Write a paragraph explaining what you understand to be the meaning of Othello's words here and why they might be considered to be significant in the context of the whole play.

3 The dying swan (in pairs)

Find out what you can of the legend that swans sing as they die. Talk together about how Emilia's image of the swan (line 245) adds to the atmosphere of this final scene.

---

coxcomb fool
precious a term used to intensify abuse
whipster whippersnapper, youngster
bode foretell

play the swan sing on the point of death
ice-brook's temper steel strengthened by being plunged into an icy stream
naked unarmed

EMILIA She give it Cassio! No, alas, I found it
         And I did give't my husband.
IAGO   Filth, thou liest!
EMILIA By heaven, I do not, I do not, gentlemen.   230
         O murderous coxcomb, what should such a fool
         Do with so good a wife?
OTHELLO   Are there no stones in heaven
         But what serves for the thunder? Precious villain!
         [Othello runs at Iago; Montano disarms him; Iago stabs Emilia from
                              behind and exit.]
GRATIANO The woman falls; sure he hath killed his wife.
EMILIA Ay, ay; O, lay me by my mistress' side.   235
GRATIANO He's gone, but his wife's killed.
MONTANO 'Tis a notorious villain. Take you this weapon,
         Which I have here recovered from the Moor.
         Come guard the door without; let him not pass,
         But kill him rather. I'll after the same villain,   240
         For 'tis a damnèd slave.
                         Exeunt Montano and Gratiano
OTHELLO   I am not valiant neither,
         But every puny whipster gets my sword.
         But why should honour outlive honesty?
         Let it go all.
EMILIA   What did thy song bode, lady?
         Hark, canst thou hear me? I will play the swan   245
         And die in music: [Sings] 'Willow, willow, willow.'
         Moor, she was chaste; she loved thee, cruel Moor;
         So come my soul to bliss, as I speak true;
         So speaking as I think, I die, I die.   She dies
OTHELLO I have another weapon in this chamber;   250
         It was a sword of Spain, the ice-brook's temper.
         O, here it is. – Uncle, I must come forth.
GRATIANO (Within) If thou attempt it, it will cost thee dear;
         Thou hast no weapon, and perforce must suffer.
OTHELLO Look in upon me then, and speak with me,   255
         Or naked as I am, I will assault thee.

Othello, now fully realising he has murdered an innocent woman, looks forward to the punishments of hell. Lodovico and the others return with Iago and Othello attacks him.

---

1 Othello imagines his fate (in groups of four or five)

Lines 257–79 comprise three distinct but connected parts, corresponding with the three stages of Othello's life: Othello the great warrior, Othello the murderer at his life's end, and Othello tortured in hell. Underlying his life's journey, imagined as a sea voyage, he feels there is a strong element of fate controlling events.

Find the three elements of the speech. Make a group presentation, exploring the structure of the speech and its images.

2 Lodovico's entrance (in groups of seven or eight)

With the entrance of Lodovico and Cassio, the controlling force of Venetian law is reintroduced. Lodovico calls on the two defendants as if in a court of law, and presides as if a high court judge.

Work out how you would stage the entrance of Lodovico and the others following the script from line 275 to the bottom of the page. Explore the most effective way to position everyone in the space available to you.

If you prefer to work on your own, plot the moves and positioning for the same lines, using the plan of an Elizabethan theatre on page 186. Write a paragraph justifying your choices.

---

your stop your force as a guard
butt goal, target
sea-mark beacon
man but a rush aim just a reed

ill-starred ill-fated
compt the Day of Judgement
his feet ... fable (the devil was
  supposed to have cloven feet)

[*Enter Gratiano.*]

GRATIANO What is the matter?

OTHELLO   Behold, I have a weapon:
A better never did itself sustain
Upon a soldier's thigh. I have seen the day   260
That with this little arm and this good sword
I have made my way through more impediments
Than twenty times your stop. But, O vain boast!
Who can control his fate? 'Tis not so now.
Be not afraid, though you do see me weaponed:
Here is my journey's end, here is my butt   265
And very sea-mark of my utmost sail.
Do you go back dismayed? 'Tis a lost fear:
Man but a rush against Othello's breast,
And he retires. Where should Othello go?
      [*He goes to the bed.*]
Now, how dost thou look now? O ill-starred wench!   270
Pale as thy smock! When we shall meet at compt
This look of thine will hurl my soul from heaven
And fiends will snatch at it. Cold, cold, my girl,
Even like thy chastity.
O cursèd, cursèd slave! Whip me, ye devils,   275
From the possession of this heavenly sight!
Blow me about in winds! Roast me in sulphur!
Wash me in steep-down gulfs of liquid fire!
O Desdemon! Dead Desdemon! Dead! O! O!

Enter LODOVICO, *Montano,* CASSIO *in a chair, Iago in the charge of*
OFFICERS.

LODOVICO Where is this rash and most unfortunate man?   280
OTHELLO That's he that was Othello: here I am.
LODOVICO Where is that viper? Bring the villain forth.
OTHELLO I look down towards his feet; but that's a fable.
      If that thou be'st a devil, I cannot kill thee.
            [*He wounds Iago.*]

Lodovico takes control and investigates the case. Othello asks Cassio's pardon. Letters found in Roderigo's pockets tell of Iago's plot to kill Cassio and of Roderigo's threat to expose Iago. Iago refuses to give any explanation of his conduct.

1 How?

Iago's line, 'I bleed, sir, but not killed' could be uttered in a variety of ways. How would you advise an actor to say those words? Consider the following suggestions to help you make your decision:

- Iago is playing for sympathy
- he is bitterly sarcastic
- he is resigned to his fate
- he is detached and neutral
- he is utterly defeated, in pain and wants to die
- he is triumphant, taunting Othello
- he is chillingly inhuman, hinting at his own indestructibility.

2 And why?

Why does Iago refuse to speak further? Write a paragraph to explain his silence.

3 'An honourable murderer . . .' (in pairs)

Othello claims that he is 'an honourable murderer . . . For naught did I in hate, but all in honour'. How do you think Othello might defend this statement? Role-play an imaginary interview between Lodovico and Othello where this conversation is extended.

4 The letters

Two letters are found in Roderigo's possession, both helping to explain Iago's plotting. The first is probably written by Iago and 'imports the death of Cassio'. The second is a 'discontented paper' written by Roderigo, but is it to Iago or Othello? Write the two letters.

---

torments torture
in the nick in the nick of time

satisfied him stopped his complaints
caitiff wretch, villain

LODOVICO Wrench his sword from him.

IAGO   I bleed, sir, but not killed.   285

OTHELLO I am not sorry neither; I'd have thee live,
          For in my sense 'tis happiness to die.

LODOVICO O, thou Othello, that wert once so good,
          Fallen in the practice of a damnèd slave,
          What shall be said to thee?

OTHELLO   Why, anything: 290
          An honourable murderer, if you will;
          For naught did I in hate, but all in honour.

LODOVICO This wretch hath part confessed his villainy.
          Did you and he consent in Cassio's death?

OTHELLO Ay.   295

CASSIO Dear general, I never gave you cause.

OTHELLO I do believe it, and I ask your pardon.
          Will you, I pray, demand that demi-devil
          Why he hath thus ensnared my soul and body?

IAGO Demand me nothing; what you know, you know.   300
          From this time forth I never will speak word.

LODOVICO What! Not to pray?

GRATIANO Torments will ope your lips.

OTHELLO   Well, thou dost best.

LODOVICO Sir, you shall understand what hath befallen,
          Which, as I think, you know not. Here is a letter   305
          Found in the pocket of the slain Roderigo,
          And here another: the one of them imports
          The death of Cassio, to be undertook
          By Roderigo.

OTHELLO   O villain!

CASSIO   Most heathenish and most gross!

LODOVICO Now here's another discontented paper,   310
          Found in his pocket too; and this, it seems,
          Roderigo meant to have sent this damnèd villain,
          But that, belike, Iago, in the nick,
          Came in and satisfied him.

OTHELLO   O the pernicious caitiff!
          How came you, Cassio, by that handkerchief   315
          That was my wife's?

Cassio tells of how he found the handkerchief, and of how Roderigo was used by Iago. Lodovico pronounces Othello's arrest and Cassio's instatement as governor. Othello asks that his whole story should be truthfully told. He stabs himself.

1 Punishments (in pairs)

Lodovico sentences Iago to 'cunning cruelty' and 'torment' (torture), whilst Othello is to be kept under close arrest and then tried by the Venetian courts. Decide what you would consider to be fitting punishment for the two men. Give reasons for any difference in treatment that you decide upon (including the difference in Lodovico's own sentencing).

2 Othello's obituary

Othello's last major speech in the play amounts to his own obituary. He follows the conventions of obituary writers and includes the following elements:

- his service in Venetian colonial exploits (line 335)
- his past great deeds (lines 348–52)
- his emotional/love life (line 340)
- his downfall (lines 341–4)
- his last moments (lines 344–7).

Some readers have found it difficult to accept all aspects of Othello's own interpretation of his life. He claims he 'loved not wisely, but too well' and that he was 'one not easily jealous but, being wrought, /Perplexed in the extreme'. Both could be said to be rather contentious remarks!

Write an alternative obituary. Follow the conventions of obituary writers, but write your obituary from the point of view of an 'underground' Cyprus newspaper, critical of the occupying Venetian forces. Think about how you imagine the average Cypriot citizen would regard the whole incident involving their recently appointed military leader.

---

upbraids tells off
brave insult
soft you just a moment

base Indian American Indians were famed for their 'ignorance' about the value of precious gems
traduced insulted

CASSIO   I found it in my chamber;
              And he himself confessed but even now
              That there he dropped it for a special purpose
              Which wrought to his desire.
OTHELLO   O fool, fool, fool!
CASSIO There is besides in Roderigo's letter   320
              How he upbraids Iago, that he made him
              Brave me upon the watch, whereon it came
              That I was cast; and even but now he spake –
              After long seeming dead – Iago hurt him,
              Iago set him on.   325
LODOVICO You must forsake this room and go with us.
              Your power and your command is taken off
              And Cassio rules in Cyprus. For this slave,
              If there be any cunning cruelty
              That can torment him much and hold him long   330
              It shall be his. You shall close prisoner rest
              Till that the nature of your fault be known
              To the Venetian state. Come, bring him away.
OTHELLO Soft you; a word or two before you go.
              I have done the state some service and they know't: 335
              No more of that. I pray you, in your letters
              When you shall these unlucky deeds relate,
              Speak of me as I am; nothing extenuate,
              Nor set down aught in malice. Then must you speak
              Of one that loved not wisely, but too well;   340
              Of one not easily jealous but, being wrought,
              Perplexed in the extreme; of one whose hand,
              Like the base Indian, threw a pearl away
              Richer than all his tribe; of one whose subdued eyes,
              Albeit unusèd to the melting mood,   345
              Drops tears as fast as the Arabian trees
              Their medicinable gum. Set you down this;
              And say besides that in Aleppo once
              Where a malignant and a turbaned Turk
              Beat a Venetian and traduced the state,   350
              I took by th'throat the circumcisèd dog
              And smote him thus.
                            He stabs himself.

Othello dies beside Desdemona. Lodovico awards Othello's possessions to Gratiano, and orders Cassio to decide Iago's punishment. Lodovico leaves to report in full to the Venetian State.

1 'Look on the tragic loading of this bed'
(in groups of seven to ten)

Show it!

2 Lodovico's report (in groups of four or five)

Lodovico states his intention of going immediately to Venice to make his formal report of events to the Senate. Imagine the scene and act out Lodovico delivering his report to the Duke and other senators. It would be a very formal occasion and Lodovico would probably have written his report in advance. Decide what questions the Duke and other senators would want to ask about their former 'hero'.

3 Cassio as general, Bianca as . . . ? (in pairs)

The last time we saw Bianca was when she was led off at Iago's insistence just after Cassio had been injured. Imagine that Cassio now encounters her as he leaves Othello's house. How would the new general of the occupying force react? Improvise the scene.

4 A final image

What last image would you want an audience to be left with in a production of *Othello*? The final stage direction (*exeunt*) is for all the remaining actors to go off, but there are several choices for a director to make. Would you have them all leaving together? Would you want the bodies on the bed to be spotlit or obscured by curtains? Might you wish to end with a tableau involving all or some of the remaining characters? Discuss, and show your final image.

---

period conclusion
Spartan dog the legendary hounds of Sparta in Greece were extremely savage

fell cruel
censure judgement

LODOVICO O bloody period!

GRATIANO   All that's spoke is marred!

OTHELLO I kissed thee ere I killed thee: no way but this,

Killing myself, to die upon a kiss.   355

                              He [falls on the bed and] dies

CASSIO This did I fear, but thought he had no weapon,

For he was great of heart.

LODOVICO [*To Iago*]   O Spartan dog,

More fell than anguish, hunger, or the sea,

Look on the tragic loading of this bed:

This is thy work. The object poisons sight;   360

Let it be hid.

                    [*The bed-curtains are drawn.*]

                         Gratiano, keep the house

And seize upon the fortunes of the Moor,

For they succeed on you. To you, lord governor,

Remains the censure of this hellish villain:

The time, the place, the torture, O, enforce it!   365

Myself will straight aboard, and to the state

This heavy act with heavy heart relate.

                                             Exeunt

Looking back at the whole play

1 Fifteen-minute version

Divide yourselves into five groups, each group taking one act of the play. You are going to produce a three-minute version of your chosen act, only using words from the script itself. When you are ready, put each of the five acts together in turn: you have created a fifteen-minute version of the whole play!

As a variation, mime or perform each act in a different style (soap opera, documentary investigation, slapstick comedy, melodrama, etc.).

2 Photographs (in pairs)

Create a 'photograph' of Iago with one other character. The second person's identity should be obvious from their posture, position, and facial expressions. Show your photograph. The rest of the class guess Iago's companion.

3 Production matters

Imagine you are producing *Othello*.

a At what point in the play would you have the interval?
b What music would you play as the audience took their seats at the start, or as they left at the end?
c Design a poster, other publicity material ('flyers') and programme cover.
d Write the programme notes for your production.
e Draw up a cast list, indicating which male characters could 'double up' their parts.

4 Coroner's investigation (written version)

Three or four corpses, one suicide and three suspected murders all in the space of one evening! The coroner in Cyprus would be kept busy investigating the full circumstances of each of the deaths. Compile the coroner's dossier. It includes eye-witness statements, psychiatric reports, post-mortem reports, and any other relevant documentation about the deceased. Include mock-ups of Army personnel files, newspaper cuttings and personal letters. Use your imagination! Work in small groups and produce a large display of the various examples of written 'evidence'. (See also pages 222–3.)

5 Film trailer (in groups of five)

Imagine a new film version of *Othello* is about to be launched. Create a 'trailer' to publicise the film, consisting of voice-over, advertising 'hype' and a selection of short 'clips' from the film.

6 Book launch

You are a publicity agent for a publishing company. Create a series of press releases to publicise the launch of a new edition of *Othello*, aimed at the following markets:

English teachers
National Schools Examinations Boards
Youth Theatre Groups
teenagers
a Council for Racial Equality.

7 Adaptation – a happy ending

In the eighteenth century it was popular to rewrite certain of Shakespeare's tragedies (*Romeo and Juliet*, *King Lear*) in order to give them a happy ending. You are a stage adapter and have been asked to give *Othello* a happy ending. How will you do it? Outline your alterations with some examples of your new script.

8 Settings

What setting would you choose for a modern version of *Othello*? The 1971 and 1989 Royal Shakespeare Company productions were set in far-flung colonies of the British Empire in the nineteenth century. Productions of *Macbeth* have been set as an American gangster film, a Japanese Samurai epic, a science-fiction story, a modern city business environment. What suitable settings of the past, present or future might you choose for your own production of *Othello*? Design a stage set and costumes to go with your choice.

9 Roderigo's story

Amazingly, Roderigo is not dead after all (5.2.323–4)! Ten years later, Roderigo tells his story . . .

Coroner's investigation
A role-play activity for the whole class

Time: a month after Othello's death.
Place: a coroner's court in Venice.
This group activity will help you revise your knowledge and understanding of the whole play. Create a whole class role-play around an imaginary coroner's investigation. It provides plenty of scope for getting everyone imaginatively involved in an active investigation of characters' relationships, motivations and the public and private aspects of the play.

The following notes will help focus each participant's preparation for the role-play. Take time to prepare your character and their side of the story, then set the room out as a court. The Coroner presides over the hearing and assesses the evidence at the end of the role-play.

Coroner
- work in a small group with the assistant / usher(s), etc.
- what questions will you put to each character?
- what concrete evidence exists? Any exhibits to use in court (for example, weapons / letters, etc.)?
- consider how you will shape your questions to elicit full answers (as opposed to 'yes' / 'no' replies)

Coroner's assistant
- assist Coroner in running the proceedings
- establish an order of events and present it on paper

Montano
- what contact did you have with Othello / Cassio / Iago? Impressions?
- any important/significant events you witnessed first hand?
- did Othello live up to his reputation?

Duke of Venice
- how will you behave in court?
- which characters did you know well?
- what relevant evidence do you have for the court?
- how do you see your position in relation to the whole Cyprus venture now?
- do you feel any responsibility for what has happened?

Iago

- will you offer any defence? Why might you be persuaded to talk?
- what motivation exists for your acts? (look up your major speeches and soliloquies).
- why do you think Cassio got the job of Othello's second-in-command instead of you?
- what do you think of other characters?

Lodovico

- what is your considered opinion about the cause of the deaths?
- what do you think of Othello's behaviour in the time you knew him?
- what relevant events were you present at?
- how do you see your position in relation to the whole Cyprus venture?

Bianca

- what contact did you have with any of the main characters?
- were there any significant events you witnessed first hand?
- what do you feel about the tragic events?
- how do you regard your position in this society?

Roderigo

- yes - you live! (see 5.2.323-4) - though you might be walking with difficulty
- your meetings with Iago
- your part in his plots
- what you now think of Iago, Desdemona, Cassio, Othello
- what you said to Cassio before the brawl
- where you've been for the past month

Cassio

- what is your version of events?
- who seems to blame?
- what is your opinion of Othello now?
- what was Othello like to serve under?
- why did you get promoted over Iago?
- what do you look forward to?

A Gentleman of Cyprus

- at what important event were you present?
- why were you there?
- give your version of the occasion
- what is your reaction to the tragic deaths, and how do you feel about the continuation of Venetian rule?

Clown

- who employed you?
- what messages were you given and to whom were you sent?
- what was your impression of the people you came into contact with?
- how would you describe their changing moods?
- consider how you might act/speak in court (terrible puns, for instance?)

Gratiano

- how do you feel about the deaths of your brother and niece? How have your family in Venice reacted?
- could you have done anything to prevent the tragedy?
- what eye-witness accounts can you offer the court?

Other roles (if needed) Jury members, court ushers - could be involved in helping others to prepare their roles, or be responsible for creating exhibits (letters, etc.).

'Far more fair than black'

Language, race and culture in the play

On page 12, you were asked to explore the way language carries and reinforces the prejudices of the dominant social group. It's easy to recognise the blatant and intentional racist abuse in much of Iago's and Roderigo's dialogue ('the thick-lips', or 'an old black ram/Is tupping your white ewe'). But language often works more subtly in carrying meaning. Pages 224–6 extend the activity from page 12 and explore more fully how language may be culturally loaded.

1 Definitions (in pairs)

Look up the word 'black' in a dictionary. Note down how many different uses there are of the word. Now do the same for 'white' and 'fair'. Divide the definitions into *positive* and *negative* uses. If you look up these words in the Oxford English Dictionary, in your school or college library, you could also research the earliest recorded dates of particular usages. Discuss your findings with the whole class, making links and comparisons between the three sets of definitions.

2 Meanings

Discuss in what sense the Duke is using the word 'black' in:

'If virtue no delighted beauty lack
Your son-in-law is far more fair than black.'   (1.3.285–6)

Then talk together about how you think Othello is intending 'black' to be interpreted in the following two examples:

'. . . Her name, that was as fresh
As Dian's visage, is now begrimed and black
As mine own face . . .'   (3.3.387–9)

'Arise black vengeance . . .'   (3.3.448)

Identify other uses of black in the play and discuss their meanings in the context of who uses the word, and when.

3 Portrayals (in pairs)

The conventional image of hell is of a place of evil and torture, darkness and hopelessness, with the devil as the embodiment of all of these. Consider Emilia's line:

'. . . O, the more angel she,
And you the blacker devil!'   (5.2.132–3)

Does it fit your own picture of hell?

In Shakespeare's *Macbeth* the three witches are called 'secret, black and midnight hags', and the tyrant Macbeth himself is referred to as 'black Macbeth'. 'The devil damn thee black' is hurled as a curse upon a servant. Here, blackness is linked strongly with evil.

How many similar references can you find in *Othello* which link blackness with the devil?

4 Other writers (in pairs)

Consider the following poems and compare their usage of the word 'black' with that in *Othello*.

White Lies

Humming Maggie.
Hit by a virus,
the Caucasian Craze,
sees horror in the mirror.
Frantic and dutifully
she corrodes a sooty face,
braves a hot iron comb
on a shrubby scalp.
I look on.

I know pure white,
a white heart,
white, peace, ultimate virtue.
Angels are white
angels are good.
Me I'm black,
black as sin stuffed in a snuff-tin.
Lord, I've been brainwhitewashed.

But for Heaven's sake God,
just let me be.
Under cover of my darkness
let me crusade.
On a canvas stretching from here
to Dallas, Memphis, Belsen, Golgotha,
I'll daub a white devil.
Let me teach black truth.
That dark clouds aren't a sign of doom,
but hope. Rain. Life.
Let me unleash a volty bolt of black,
so all around may know black right.

Stanley Mogoba (South Africa, 1973)

The Little Black Boy

My mother bore me in the southern wild,
And I am black, but O! my soul is white;
White as an angel is the English child,
But I am black, as if bereav'd of light.

My mother taught me underneath a tree,
And sitting down before the heat of day,
She took me on her lap and kissed me,
And pointing to the east, began to say:

'Look on the rising sun: there God does live,
'And gives his light, and gives his heat away;
'And flowers and trees and beasts and men receive
'Comfort in morning, joy in the noonday.

'And we are put on earth a little space,
'That we may learn to bear the beams of love;
'And these black bodies and this sunburnt face
'Is but a cloud, and like a shady grove.

'For when our souls have learn'd the heat to bear,
'The cloud will vanish; we shall hear his voice,
'Saying: "Come out from the grove, my love and care,
'"And round my gold tent like lambs rejoice."'

Thus did my mother say, and kissed me;
And thus I say to little English boy.
When I from black and he from white cloud free,
And round the tent of God like lambs we joy,

I'll shade him from the heat, till he can bear
To lean in joy upon our father's knee;
And then I'll stand and stroke his silver hair,
And be like him, and he will then love me.

William Blake (England, 1789)

Is *Othello* a racist play?

The central character of the play could be said to be:

- mentally unstable
- physically aggressive
- sensual
- insanely jealous
- highly gullible.

His main action in the play is to:

- strangle a white woman.

He is black.

A clear example of offensive racial stereotyping?

Certainly, there is plenty of historical evidence of racial stereotyping in Elizabethan England. There were enough black residents (mainly from the African continent) to prompt Elizabeth I to express her discontent at the great numbers of 'Negars and blackamoors which are crept into the realm . . .'. Travel writers portrayed the natives of Africa as barbarous, lawless and 'a people of beastly lyvinge'. One contemporary writer on the history and people of Africa claimed that 'whomsoever they finde but talking with their wives they presently go about to murther them . . . by reason of jealousie you may see them daily one to be the death and destruction of another . . .' (from Eldred Jones, *Othello's Countrymen*, 1965).

What the critics say

In 1693, Thomas Rymer published *A Short View of Tragedy*. He saw the moral of *Othello*, to be 'a caution of all Maidens of Quality how, without their parents' consent, they run away with Blackamoors'. He goes on to draw comparisons between the imagined Venetian society of the play and his own seventeenth-century England: 'With us a Blackamoor might rise to be a trumpeter . . . With us a Moor might marry some little drab, or Small-coal Wench . . . certaynly never was any Play fraught like this of *Othello* with improbabilities.'

Just over a century later, Samuel Taylor Coleridge, expresses a similar view: 'It would be something monstrous to conceive this beautiful Venetian girl falling in love with a veritable negro.'

Many influential twentieth-century writers on *Othello* have concentrated on debating Othello's precise ethnic origins, taking great pains to prove that Othello would have been Arabic in appearance. A.C. Bradley (*Shakespearean Tragedy*, 1904) explains what he saw to be the importance of this point: 'Perhaps if we saw Othello coal-black with the bodily eye, the aversion of our blood . . . would overpower our imagination'. (See the cover illustration for what Bradley probably had in mind.)

F.R. Leavis (*The Common Pursuit*, 1952) ascribes 'voluptuous sensuality', and 'sensual possessiveness, appetite . . .' to the central character, and comments that 'the stuff of which he is made begins . . . to deteriorate and show itself unfit'.

Are they right to read the play in this way?

Culture and identity

Discuss the representation of different cultural groups in the play. The following questions may help focus your attention on some particularly salient points:

Which characters express racist sentiments in the play?
Who is presented as being an evil influence in the play?
Is Othello the only character duped by Iago?
Who or what destroys Othello's marriage?
Who speaks the richest poetry in the play?
Which characters unwaveringly admire Othello?
Which characters might be seen to have the highest moral code?
Which characters could be said to be amoral (non-moral)?
Some characters believe in fidelity, romantic ideals – who are they?
Who are the characters cynically rejecting romantic notions of love?
What do you see as the main cause of Othello's insecurity?
Which characters base their actions on a firm belief in Justice, Honesty and Trust as ideals?

Why might some people claim the play is about alienation and belonging?
Does social class have any importance?
How are outward appearances misleading in the play?
Would Shakespeare's audience immediately have disliked Othello because he is black? If so, what kind of play is it?

After your discussion:

Either: design on large sheets of paper, a diagrammatic way of recording your ideas on culture and race in the play (use bar graphs, flow diagrams, spider diagrams, imagery from the play, realistic, or stylised drawings). Present your finished display to the rest of the class.

Or: find a way of presenting your ideas through oral and/or dramatic means. Use role-play, improvisation, tableaux, or choral speaking of collected extracts and quotations. Record your presentation on audio/video tape/photographs.

After each group has completed their presentation, make a display of all illustrative material.

Two black actors in the role of Othello.

It's a man's world!

Nowhere in Shakespeare are relations between males and females more searchingly, painfully probed.   (Marilyn French, 1982)

There are only three women in the play: Desdemona, Emilia and Bianca. Each one is bound up in a relationship with a man. Only one survives.

How are these women represented in the play? What are their roles and how restricted are they by their society?

Working in small groups, consider the roles of the three women. Use this list of statements to discuss in turn, deciding which you agree or disagree with:

All three women are presented according to *men's* interpretations.
The women are completely passive.
Each woman is defined in terms of her male partner.
Women are fully emancipated in the play.
Each woman stands for an aspect of 'womanhood' – romantic idealist, practical realist and sex object.
Each relationship provokes jealousy in one partner.
Women's roles in the play are ambiguous.
The women are all portrayed as being rather stupid.
Men hold all the power in Venetian society.
Each woman comes from a different social class and that is significant.
Women talk the most sense in the play.
The women are bonded by some notion of 'sisterhood'.
The women are more trusting than men.
Men use abusive terms to refer to women; women don't use abusive terms back.
All three women have identical attitudes to men and relationships.

Choose two or three quotations from the play which seem to say something important about the presentation of one or all of the women characters. Put the lines together into a short oral, dramatic or written presentation which sums up your conclusions.

Ellen Terry as
Desdemona (1881).

Bianca and Cassio
(Royal Shakespeare
Company, 1989).

Iago and Emilia (Royal Shakespeare Company, 1989).

Critics' forum

On these two pages are extracts from influential *Othello* critics of the twentieth century. Also included are some very recent ideas of the play. You will discover that the readings offered are very different, in some cases quite contradictory. Working in small groups, read through each extract and discuss what evidence from the play the particular writer in each case might be using to support his or her view. Try to suggest what other influences each reader brings to their interpretation of the play (for instance, Christian beliefs, feminism, etc.).

The next part of the activity is a challenging one, but really rewarding – and fun in the process! Imagine 'Critics' Forum' is a late evening television arts programme, chaired by Melanie Bookworm. In it, a group of professional critics with very differing views are put together for a discussion on a particular work of literature. Tonight it is *Othello*. One student (as Ms Bookworm) chairs the debate, the rest choose a critical stance from the extracts given, and each argues their case! Remember, you have to know the play really well and you'll have to do thorough preparation beforehand.

He does not belong to our world, and he seems to enter it we know not whence – almost as if from wonderland. There is something mysterious in his descent from men of royal siege; in his wanderings in vast deserts and among marvellous peoples; in his tales of magic handkerchiefs and prophetic Sibyls; in the sudden vague glimpses we get of numberless battles and sieges in which he has played the hero and has borne a charmed life; even in chance references to his baptism, his being sold to slavery, his sojourn in Aleppo.

And he is not merely a romantic figure; his own nature is romantic.

So he comes before us, dark and grand, with a light upon him from the sun where he was born.

(A.C. Bradley, 1904)

Among the tragedies of Shakespeare *Othello* is supreme in one quality: beauty. Much of its poetry, in imagery, perfection of phrase, and steadiness of rhythm, soaring yet firm, enchants the sensuous imagination.

Othello is like a hero of the ancient world in that he is not a man like us, but a man recognised as extraordinary. He seems born to do great deeds and live in legend. He has the heroic capacity for passion. But the thing which most sets him apart is his solitariness. He is a stranger, a man of alien race, without ties of nature or natural duties. He is, in a sense, a 'self-made man', the product of a certain kind of life which he has chosen to lead.

(Helen Gardner, 1955)

Two different kinds of love are movingly displayed here. Othello's is the masculine and romantic: his opening hyperbole invokes the romantic commonplace – 'Love calls to war'– and also receives Desdemona into his wholly martial personality, just as she had wished in refusing to remain 'a moth of peace'. The glory of the achievement is carried buoyantly on in the image of the ship riding the waves. What battles and dangers wouldn't they undergo for this? But then with the imagined calm a note of brooding appears; the tone changes and deepens; 'If it were now to die. . . .' Othello has withdrawn his delighted gaze from Desdemona and is addressing himself and his own vision of love. And in the romantic context that vision has an alarming familiarity. Having achieved his desire, Othello turns naturally to the idea of the *Liebestod*, death as the only fit and comparable peer of love. How can the tension otherwise be kept up and the lover remain at the summit of his happiness? Unknowingly Othello is applying this fatal romantic logic.

(John Bayley, 1962)

In loving and marrying each other, Othello and Desdemona instinctively act according to principles of racial equality and sexual freedom which are still not normative, still far from generally accepted and practised even in our own day, let alone in Shakespeare's.

Shakespeare's tragic protagonists are all overpowered by the prevailing social and ideological tides which sweep them unawares out of their depth, rather than by some metaphysically predestined misfortune or by some flaw, whether culpable, haphazard or innate, in the composition of their characters.

(Kiernan Ryan, 1989)

The action of *Othello* opens out to include the audience, and their perception of the struggle of good and evil. They do not go home hoping they will never meet an Iago, but rather understanding something of the nature of evil and how soon bright things come to confusion. The ethical notion of evil as defective, absurd, and inconsistent is Aristotelian, but the embodiment of these characteristics in an agent, which makes possible the dynamic presentation of evil as an active force, is Christian. We no longer feel, as Shakespeare's contemporaries did, the ubiquity of Satan, but Iago is still serviceable to us, as an objective correlative of the mindless inventiveness of racist aggression. Iago is still alive and kicking and filling migrants' letterboxes with excrement.

(Germaine Greer, 1986)

Othello, in his magnanimous way, is egotistic. He really is, beyond any question, the nobly massive man of action, the captain of men, he sees himself as being, but he does very much see himself:

Keep up our bright swords, for the dew will rust them.

In short, a habit of self-approving, self-dramatisation is an essential element in Othello's make-up, and remains so at the very end.

It is, at the best, the impressive manifestation of a noble egotism. But, in the new marital situation, this egotism isn't going to be the less dangerous for its nobility. This self-centredness doesn't mean self-knowledge: that is a virtue which Othello, as soldier of fortune, hasn't had much need of.

(F.R. Leavis, 1952)

So, what is *Othello* about?

As you worked on some of the activities in this edition it will have become very clear to you that there are a number of possible readings of *Othello*. The traditional way of reading a Shakespeare tragedy is to examine the text for what it would reveal about characters, particularly the hero. Critics have applied ancient Greek ideas on Tragedy (Aristotle, for example) and assume that the tragic hero is always presented as having a mixture of admirable qualities and a 'tragic flaw' which proves fatal. The hero's fall from grace should move the audience to pity and fear.

However, there are problems with such readings. There is evidence that the Elizabethan playwrights were not concerned with constructing psychologically consistent 'characters'. Indeed, it seems that the fascination with tragic heroes emerged some time during the nineteenth century – the time of the great Victorian actor-managers, famed for their starring roles. Also, some critics and historians have suggested that Victorian moralists were interested in using Shakespeare's characters as examples for moral guidance.

In small groups, discuss how you might apply the idea of the tragically-flawed noble hero to Othello. What 'moral lesson' might a Victorian reader be tempted to draw from the play? Using this line of interpretation, how do you explain Desdemona and Emilia's deaths?

But, if recent critics have rejected the overriding importance of character in Shakespeare's tragedies, what alternative reading are they offering? There seems to be some evidence that Elizabethan audiences were also concerned with interplay between characters, and the interchange of ideas in the plays. Shakespeare was writing at a time of rapid change socially, politically and economically. Feudalism was giving way to capitalism; there were attacks on the crown: in 1605, one year after *Othello* was first performed, a group of plotters tried to assassinate the king and all the members of government in the Gunpowder Plot; and, only twenty-five or so years after Shakespeare's death, civil war broke out in England and the king was subsequently executed.

In small groups discuss what possibilities there are for interpreting *Othello* as a play about social change, political or cultural values. Do these readings better account for any inconsistencies in the plot or 'characterisation'?

The Moorish Ambassador to Queen Elizabeth I (1600–1). Compare this picture of a 'noble Moor' with other illustrations of Othello in this edition.

William Shakespeare 1564–1616

1564 Born Stratford-upon-Avon, eldest son of John and Mary Shakespeare.
1582 Married to Anne Hathaway of Shottery, near Stratford.
1583 Daughter, Susanna, born.
1585 Twins, son and daughter, Hamnet and Judith, born.
1592 First mention of Shakespeare in London. Robert Greene, another playwright, described Shakespeare as 'an upstart crow beautified with our feathers . . .'. Greene seems to have been jealous of Shakespeare. He mocked Shakespeare's name, calling him 'the only Shake-scene in the country' (presumably because Shakespeare was writing successful plays).
1595 A shareholder in 'The Lord Chamberlain's Men', an acting company that became extremely popular.
1596 Son Hamnet died, aged 11.
     Father, John, granted arms (acknowledged as a gentleman).
1597 Bought New Place, the grandest house in Stratford.
1598 Acted in Ben Jonson's *Every Man in His Humour*.
1599 Globe Theatre opens on Bankside. Performances in the open air.
1601 Father, John, dies.
1603 James I granted Shakespeare's company a royal patent: 'The Lord Chamberlain's Men' became 'The King's Men' and played about twelve performances each year at court.
1607 Daughter, Susanna, marries Dr John Hall.
1608 Mother, Mary, dies.
1609 'The King's Men' begin performing indoors at Blackfriars Theatre.
1610 Probably returned from London to live in Stratford.
1616 Daughter, Judith, marries Thomas Quiney.
     Died. Buried in Holy Trinity Church, Stratford-upon-Avon.

The plays and poems

(no one knows exactly when he wrote each play)

1589–1595 *The Two Gentlemen of Verona, The Taming of the Shrew, First, Second and Third Parts of King Henry VI, Titus Andronicus, King Richard III, The Comedy of Errors, Love's Labour's Lost, A Midsummer Night's Dream, Romeo and Juliet, King Richard II* (and the long poems *Venus and Adonis* and *The Rape of Lucrece*).

1596–1599 *King John, The Merchant of Venice, First and Second Parts of King Henry IV, The Merry Wives of Windsor, Much Ado About Nothing, King Henry V, Julius Caesar* (and probably the *Sonnets*).

1600–1605 *As You Like It, Hamlet, Twelfth Night, Troilus and Cressida, Measure for Measure, Othello, All's Well That Ends Well, Timon of Athens, King Lear.*

1606–1611 *Macbeth, Antony and Cleopatra, Pericles, Coriolanus, The Winter's Tale, Cymbeline, The Tempest.*

1613 *King Henry VIII, The Two Noble Kinsmen* (both probably with John Fletcher).

1623 Shakespeare's plays published as a collection (now called the First Folio).